CLIVE FRANCIS
is well known as an actor as well as a caricaturist. He has made over a hundred television appearances and performed in over twenty West End productions including *There's a Girl in My Soup*, *The Return of A.J. Raffles*, *Bloomsbury*, *The Circle*, *Look After Lulu*, *The Rear Column*, *The School For Scandal*, *The Importance of Being Ernest*, *Benefactors*, *What the Butler Saw*, *Single Spies*, *Absolute Turkey* and earlier this year, *Entertaining Mr Sloane*. He appeared in *A Small Family Business* for Alan Ayckbourn at the Royal National Theatre and recently completed a season for the Royal Shakespeare Company: *Three Hours After Marriage*, *Troilus and Cressida* and Ebenezer Scrooge in *A Christmas Carol*.

Clive Francis began caricaturing professionally in 1983 and has had seven solo exhibitions including three at the National Theatre. He has designed a number of posters and book covers, including two for Alec Guinness and two for John Gielgud. His first book of theatrical caricatures, *Laugh Lines*, was published in 1989, and in 1994, to coinside with Gielgud's 90th birthday, he produced for Robson Books

Last year saw the first of his
like a Thane! The lighter side

The best thing about Ian McKellen's Hamlet is his curtain call.
Harold Hobson.

There is Nothing Like a Dane!

The Lighter Side of Hamlet

Compiled and illustrated by

Clive Francis

ROBSON BOOKS

For Natalie
Harry and Lucinda
with love

I am indebted to the following for all their help and co-operation;
John Fisher, Roy Hudd, John Sessions, Edward Hardwicke, John Mortimer, Mrs
Tommy Cooper, Roger Pringle and the Shakespeare Institute Library, Stratford
University Library, The Garrick Club Library, The Theatre Museum, Westminster
Reference Library
Also I would like to thank my editor Nick Hern for so carefully helping me shape and
modify this book.

First published in Great Britain 2001 by Robson Books, 10 Blenheim Court,
London N7 9NY

British Library Cataloguing in Publication Data
A catalogue record for this title is available from the British Library.

ISBN 1 86105 459 9

Printed in Great Britain by Bell & Bain Ltd., Glasgow

Introduction

CLIVE FRANCIS

It was during the summer of 1955 that my sister Caroline and I were persuaded to enter a fancy-dress competition being organised by the local dancing school in Eastbourne. The gentle persuader was our mother Margaret, who being an ardent lover of the Bard thought that we would both stand a positive chance of winning the five shilling book token if we went as Lord Hamlet and the fair Ophelia. My sister was four, and I had just turned nine.

Even at this early age my head was swimming with thoughts of becoming an actor and playing all the great Shakespearean leads, and so the chance of dressing up as one filled me with enormous enthusiasm. Caroline, on the other hand, just did as she was told. Dressed in an old nylon nightie of my mother's she was entwined from head to toe in lengths of ivy, honeysuckle and bind-weed, with a garland of pungent parsley and rosemary neatly plaited into her hair. She looked adorably loony and was instructed when facing the judges just to 'Smile sweetly, and hum a bit!'

I wore a pair of my mother's black tights, folded over several times at the top, a huge ruffled shirt - which had just a hint of Chanel - and under my arm a skull, that my mother had borrowed from the local art college. In great trepidation of being about to look a complete burk, I walked hand in hand with my sister towards the Reeve Folkes Dancing School.

As soon as I entered the lobby, I knew I had made a mistake. I was confronted with a harem of girls in various shapes and sizes, all parading up and down in voluminous multi-coloured outfits depicting clowns, fishes, golliwogs, blancmange fairies etc; all squealing hysterically as mothers and nannies tried desperately to bring them under control.

Needless to say I wanted the ground to open up. I wanted to disappear. To evaporate. *Anything* rather than parade ruffled up to the ear-drums in a pair of wrinkly tights, with a borrowed skull and a sister unconsciously tripping over a nightie now heaving with foliage. I was aware also of a lot of young female eyes staring at us as we stood hand in hand in the corner of the hall. Not another fellow in sight, well apart from one, and he wasn't much help, as he'd come dressed as Muffin the Mule.

My mother's hand was now pressing firmly on my back, as she tried to coax us further into the hall. There was no time to lose. I needed immediately to conjure up any vestige of acting talent that might have kindled inside me, and, simply, *die*!

With a loud wail I clutched my stomach, fell to my knees and rolled writhing and wailing until I knew I had the attention of pupils and parents alike, who were now deeply concerned as to what had happened to Mrs. Francis's little boy.

My mother rushed me home and put me to bed, where, after a suitable pause, I made a remarkably quick recovery.

My sister, on the other hand, was abandoned to fend for herself. And when, after parading round the packed room, smiling and humming all the while, she was asked who she was supposed to be, said, "I don't know. But I think I'm meant to be mad!"

It is extraordinary for me to think that forty years on, my son Harry, now aged six, has also been bitten by the venomous acting bug. Shakespeare is the equivalent to him of Enid Blyton to any other child. He can, and *does*, without any coaxing, dress up in his sister's black tights, ram a red plastic oversized tomato under his arm (representing the skull of course) and perform "To be, or not to be" - although, in his case, we get "the *sling shots* and arrows of outrageous fortune!"

I saw *Hamlet* for the first time forty years ago at Croydon's Pembroke Theatre in the Round (my chief remembrance being of a lady next to me who spent most of the nunnery scene waving desperately to her friend sitting opposite.) It is, without a doubt, the most famous play ever written; certainly the most quoted and certainly the most talked about. Which is amazing when you consider that there are no jokes (well, apart from a couple; and they're rather dubious), one rather barmy song and most of the cast get bumped off by the end of Act 5. *And* it's over four hours long.

When I began compiling this book I was intrigued by the number of wild eccentrics that have essayed the role. Hamlets who have been bald, mad, foreign and short-sighted; and the odd occasion when he has been performed by ladies, puppets, dogs and undernourished children. In short the whole project became an obsession. So determined was I to track down every anecdote, parody and song ever written on the subject that my collated material began to grow to mammoth proportions. But fascinating though it all was I discovered that there weren't many laughs - which for a bleak, bitter tragedy it certainly needed. So I then began to rummage through music hall archives and theatrical libraries for amusing anecdotes and reminiscences; at the same time ceremoniously hacking away and losing at least two thirds of my original idea. This wasn't an easy task, but then there are only so many stories regarding a loony, morose, self-obsessed Prince that one can take.

It has been staged in every country in the world, on nearly every island under the sun, and, I'm sure, upon every star that twinkles within our firmament. In fact *Hamlet* has every chance of getting a reputation, unless it's very careful, of being done to death.

No offence i' the world

ACT 3, SCENE 2.

That it should come to this.
ACT 1, SCENE 2.

Imagine this

One night in a dream, the Bard of Avon hits on his finest so far and wakes himself up and quills down the necessary notes of the vision.

Next morning he reads what he has written

CASTLE SCANDINAVIA BLOKE IN TIGHTS

Ken Campbell.

Madame how like you this play?

ACT 3, SCENE 2.

Hamlet, in my opinion, is pound for pound the greatest play ever written.
Laurence Olivier.

Of course, I think it is the worst play ever written. Every actor does it out of vanity.
Peter O'Toole.

Hamlet, how boring, how boring to live with,
so mean and self-conscious, blowing and snoring,
his wonderful speeches full of other folks' whoring!
D.H. Lawrence.

Hamlet has been the darling of every country in which the literature of England has been fostered.
Samuel Taylor Coleridge.

The great, wise, and wonderful beauty of the play is a part of the English mind for ever. It is difficult to live for a day anywhere in England without hearing or reading a part of *Hamlet.*
John Masefield.

z

The readiness is all.

ACT 5, SCENE 2.

"Hamlet, Prince of Denmark; or, the Comedy in the Comedy"

Listen to Hamlet's nervous thoughts. But all of you be attentive, so that you lose nothing of their beauty by unbearable noise. Madame Godel will today, in the part of Ophelia, show the great effect of which the art of acting is capable; and Herr Godel will excite enthusiasm by his masterly acting as Hamlet; the director, in the difficult part of the Ghost, will also show himself worthy of the applause from so gracious an audience. Oh, excellent public, come and see! Then you will find what a difference it makes when *Hamlet* is played by *real* actors and not by bunglers.

A Hamburg playbill of 1776.

This bloody question...

ACT 5, SCENE 2.

Beverley Baxter, theatre critic of the *Evening Standard* in the 40's and early 50's, took an American friend to see *Hamlet* - his friend had never seen the play before. After it was over he remained silent and Baxter felt compelled to ask him what he had thought. "It was O.K. I guess. Though I wish they hadn't asked him so many Goddamn questions."

Blasted with ecstasy.

ACT 3, SCENE 1.

Sometime during the mid 1920's Fred Terry was about to open his production of *Hamlet* in the West End and invited Leslie Banks to watch the dress rehearsal with him. As soon as the curtain rose Terry fell into a deep sleep and remained comatose throughout most of the play, including a twenty-minute interval. Half way through the second half Osric appeared, played by an extremely camp young actor with multi-coloured clothes and elaborate hair. At this moment Fred Terry suddenly awoke, snorted, nudged Leslie Banks, pointed at Osric and said, "I had that woman once in Bognor Regis."

Joe and Me at the Play.

I went to the theatre Tuesday night, and did enjoy it so,
Really had the most wonderful time, I went with my cousin Joe.
My aunt came with us as chaperone, but she's as deaf as a post,
We went to see that Shakespeare thing about an old King's ghost.
Can't remember the name of the play, but I know it was terribly sad,
With a handsome young fellow all in black, who pretended he'd gone mad.
He looked so weary and wretched, I don't wonder, with such a part.
Fancy having to learn all that and saying it all by heart!
The King was dressed in a satin suit and a lovely train, all red,
And the Queen was the wife of the King and the wife of the ghost who was dead.
There was a girl in a white silk dress, with masses of golden hair,
I think she was sweet on the poor young man, but he didn't seem to care.
He carried on like a perfect brute, and went away in a rage,
Though he did come back for a kiss, and then, the next time she came on the stage,
She was carrying some lovely flowers and singing a queer old song,
And I said to Joe, you mark my words, she won't be with us long.
And sure enough, from something the Queen said to the King, I found
The poor thing was fetching more flowers when she went and got herself drowned.
They buried her, but in those days they didn't know how to behave:
The young men started fighting and jumping right into the grave.
When I am dead and laid in my grave, I do hope Joe won't jump,
He's six foot two, weighs thirteen stone, he'd come down an awful bump.
It wasn't really a cheerful play, there was too much sobbing and sighing,
Cursing and killing and praying out loud, and a horrible lot of dying.
Well, there was the ghost, to begin with, and then in another scene
The young man killed an old man who was hidden behind a screen.
The pretty girl got drowned, like I said, and the two young men they fought
Right in front of the King and Queen and the whole of the Royal Court.
The Queen died out at the back; the end was a perfect riddle.
One died here and one died there, and the nice man died in the middle.
Oh, it really was the most killing piece; but the nicest part to us
Was walking home in the moonlight (aunty went home on the bus).
And Joe was so awfully clever; he quoted out of the play.
"To be or not to be?" he said, and it's to be - next May!

Anon. (c.1890)

Speak the speech I pray you as I pronounc'd it to you trippingly on the tongue.

ACT 3, SCENE 2.

Tony Hancock *in his popular BBC television series* Hancock's Half-Hour *appeared in one episode called* The Bowmans *in June 1961. In this story he was a Walter Gabriel-type character in a radio soap opera similar to* The Archers. *Because he behaves so badly, and infuriates the rest of the cast, his character is killed off; Hancock, now out of work but wishing to cash in on his Joshua Bowman success, applies for a stage audition.*

HANCOCK (*entering the stage with small suit-case*): Hancock. Anthony Hancock. Joshua in *The Bowmans*, the every day story of simple people.
DIRECTOR (*somewhere at the back of the stalls*): Thank you. Carry on.
HANCOCK: Yes. What would you like to hear?
DIRECTOR: If it's all the same to you, we would like to hear the part that you came to audition for.
HANCOCK: I don't normally do auditions, you know.
DIRECTOR: That's all right. Carry on.

HANCOCK REMOVES HIS TRILBY. OPENS HIS CASE. AND TAKES OUT A LONG FLAXEN WIG, WHICH HE PUTS ON.

DIRECTOR: We don't need any props.
HANCOCK: Thought it might add to the charm of the whole thing. Give you some idea of how I'm going to interpret the role.
DIRECTOR: Mr. Hancock, we're quite familiar with the costume of the piece. Just get on with the reading.
HANCOCK: Certainly. Do beg your pardon. Not used to doing auditions, you know.
DIRECTOR: So you said. Now hurry along, we've got other people waiting, you know.
HANCOCK: Yes, quite. (*He trips across the stage.*)
   What light through yonder window breaks.
   'Tis Juliet and the sun is...
DIRECTOR: Mr. Hancock. The play is *Hamlet*.
HANCOCK: *Hamlet?* Is it? I was distinctly told *The Merchant of Vienna*. I'm most terribly sorry. *Hamlet* of course is a completely different cup of tea, isn't it? I mean, which interpretation do you fancy?

DIRECTOR: We just want the words loud and clear. This is a British Arts Council tour of Tanganyika. I'm sure they won't worry about the interpretation.
HANCOCK: Tanganyika? I wasn't told that.
DIRECTOR: Do you want the part, or not?
HANCOCK: It's a few weeks in the sun, I suppose. What's the money like?
DIRECTOR: Are you going to give us a reading, or not?
HANCOCK: Yes.

PAUSES. THEN BREAKS INTO HAMLET IN THE WEST COUNTRY ACCENT OF JOSHUA BOWMAN.

HANCOCK : "To be, or not to be, that be the question:
Whether 'tis nobler in the mind to suffer
The slings and arrows of outrageous fortune…"
DIRECTOR: Next!
HANCOCK: "Or to take arms against…" Pardon?
DIRECTOR: I said Tanganyika, not Norfolk. We'll let you know you later.
HANCOCK: Let me know later? I'm sorry that is not good enough.
DIRECTOR: All right, we'll let you know now. NO. Next.
HANCOCK: I feel I must remind you young man, you're not dealing with some hobbledehoy, you're dealing with an actor of some merit who just gave you the voice that captivated twenty million listeners every night for six years...
DIRECTOR: We're not interested. Next, please.
HANCOCK: I'll warn you the Tanganyikans are not going to like this. I'm very highly thought of in Dar Es Salaam. This is no way to keep the Commonwealth together. You'll be playing to empty mud huts my man. (*Exit.*)

Ray Galton and Alan Simpson.

I am thy father's spirit.

ACT 1, SCENE 5.
The goddamndest bore in literature, that pompous ass the Ghost.
John Barrymore.

I'll take the ghost's word for a thousand pound.

ACT 3, SCENE 2.
A company of impoverished players were touring the midlands during the late 1890's. They were cold and dispirited, salaries had been unpaid for quite a while, and there was much dissatisfaction in the company, so much so, that one night, when Hamlet spoke the immortal line *Perchance 'twill walk again* the door burst open and in marched the ghost, red with rage. "Walk again? Not blooming likely," he roared. "Not till 'is salary is paid 'e won't."

Incidentally did you know that the line *I am thy father's spirit,*
in Dutch, comes out as: *Ik ben de Poppaspook!*
Arthur Marshall.

I have a speech of fire.
ACT 4, SCENE 7.

After dinner, the duke says:

"Well, Capet, we'll want to make this a first-class show so I guess we'll want a little something to answer encores with. I'll answer by doing the Highland fling or the sailor's horn-pipe; and you - well, let me see - oh, I've got it - you can do Hamlet's soliloquy."

"Hamlet's which?"

"Hamlet's soliloquy, you know; the most celebrated thing in Shakespeare. Ah, it's sublime, sublime! Always fetches the house. I haven't got it in the book - I've only got one volume - but I reckon I can piece it out from memory. I'll just walk up and down a minute, and see if I can call it back from recollection's vaults."

So he went to marching up and down, thinking, and frowning horrible every now and then; then he would hoist up his eyebrows; next he would squeeze his hand on his forehead and stagger back and kind of moan; next he would sigh, and next he'd let on to drop a tear. It was beautiful to see him. By-and-by he got it. He told us to give attention... and all through his speech he howled, and spread around, and swelled up his chest, and just knocked the spots out of any acting ever *I* see before.

To be, or not to be; that is the bare bodkin
That makes calamity of so long life;
For who would fardels bear, till Birnam Wood do come to Dunsinane,
But that the fear of something after death
Murders the innocent sleep,
And makes us rather sling the arrows of outrageous fortune
Than fly to others that we know not of.
And thus the native hue of resolution, like the poor cat i' the adage,
Is sicklied o'er with care,
And all the clouds that lowered o'er our housetops,
With this regard their currents turn awry,
And lose the name of action.
'Tis a consummation devoutly to be wished. But soft you, the fair Ophelia:
Ope not thy ponderous and marble jaws,
But get thee to a nunnery - go!

Mark Twain. *Huckleberry Finn.*

O, my offence is rank, it smells to heaven.

ACT 3, SCENE 3.

One night as Donald Wolfit lay dying at the end of the play, the young actor playing Horatio knelt over him to say: "Now cracks a noble heart: good night sweet Prince...", when Wolfit looked at him and muttered, "My dear boy you must do something about your breath."

How well I remember that first *Hamlet* at Stratford, the opening of the great part-coloured curtain and the step forward to find out whether the great struggle in Hamlet's soul had really been imparted to the audience as far as I could conceive it with every fibre of my heart and brain. The audience that night and the critics the following day gave me the answer I hoped for. I had served the play honestly, and it seemed well.

Donald Wolfit. *First Interval.*

Come give us a taste of your quality: come, a passionate speech.

ACT 2, SCENE 2.

After a performance of *Othello* one evening Donald Wolfit stepped forward to address the audience at the curtain-call.

"On behalf of my company may I humbly thank you for your kind and gracious applause this evening. Your generosity has warmed our hearts and fills us with readiness for *Hamlet,* which we shall be performing for your pleasure next week. I, of course, will be taking the part of the irresolute Dane, and my dear wife, Rosalind Iden, that of Ophelia…"

At that piece of news a loud and raucous voice from the gallery shouted,

"Rosalind *bloody* Iden! She's rubbish!"

"Nevertheless," continued Wolfit, without flinching, "she will be appearing as the fair Ophelia."

Good my lord, will you see the players well bestowed?

ACT 2, SCENE 2.

Richard Burbage *(Talking to Shakespeare):* I've been thinking.
I'd like to play a Dane - young, intellectual - I see him pale, vacillating, but above
everything sad and prone to soliloquy.
Caryl Brahms & S.J.Simon. *No Bed for Bacon.*

He's gone, and with him what a world are dead,
Friends, every one, and what a blank instead;
Take him for all in all he was a man
Not to be match'd, and no age ever can.
No more young Hamlet, though but scant of breath,
Shall cry "revenge!" for his dear father's death.

**An elegy published shortly after
Richard Burbage's death, on 11 March 1618.**

Let the bloat King tempt you again to bed.

ACT 3, SCENE 4.

Kenneth Branagh *remembers his first day's rehearsal when he played Laertes opposite the Hamlet of Roger Rees at Stratford in 1984. Brian Blessed was Claudius and Virginia McKenna, Gertrude the Queen.*

Brian Blessed had come to the R.S.C. very humble about his relationship to the classics; he was a mature, successful actor who still wanted very much to learn. He was always asking, in a very direct way, "What are the rules of Shakespeare?" A big one that.

On our first morning he offered his thoughts on Claudius. Up to this point everyone had been very timid in the face of Ron's [*Ron Daniels, the director*] intellect. Brian started to develop some of Ron's ideas about the character, but quickly reverted to a rather more dynamic approach.

"The thing is Ron, I believe that… basically, when you look at this man and, you know, begin to wonder what made him tick…"

"Yes?"

Brian was clearly burning to say it. He shot a quick glance at Virginia, who sat beaming at him with her English-rose fragility. He decided to plunge in.

"Well, the thing is… he just wants to fuck her." I clenched my buttocks on Virginia's behalf. Although Virginia is not at all prudish, this was her first day at the R.S.C. and her first experience of Brian's rehearsal style. I adored Brian, but I sensed this was perhaps not the best opening line, however true it might be about Claudius. "He just can't keep his bloody hands off her. In the palace, in the garden, in the bloody kitchen. He's wild for her, she's in his blood and every time he sees her he wants to give her one."

It seemed that Brian had finished. I looked for relief on Virginia's face. I thought we were over the worst.

"And the thing is…" - oh, Christ - "she fucking *loves* it."

Kenneth Branagh. *Beginning.*

Kenneth Branagh in his own film version, which was longer than
Gone With the Wind.

Season your admiration for a while.

ACT 1, SCENE 2.

Thomas Betterton *performed Hamlet at Lincoln's Inn Fields in the Spring of 1661 - the first time that scenery was ever used for this play.*

Betterton was immensely powerful in the role, and was renowned for actually turning white when he met the Ghost in Act 1. His fellow actor, Barton Booth, on one occasion, was powerless to speak for several moments. "Instead of my awing *him*," Booth later recalled, "he terrified *me*."

> **A** shabby fellow chanced one day to meet
> The British Roscius in the street,
> Garrick, of whom our nation justly brags;
> The fellow hugged him with a kind embrace; -
> 'Good sir, I do not recollect your face,'
> Quoth Garrick. 'No?' replied the man of rags;
> 'The boards of Drury Lane you and I have trod
> Full many a time together, I am sure.'
> 'When?' with an oath, cried Garrick, 'for by God,
> I never saw that face of yours before!
> What characters, I pray,
> Did you and I together play?'
> 'Lord!' quoth the fellow, 'think not that I mock -
> When you played Hamlet, sir, I played the cock!'
> **John Pindar. 1786.**

Tears in his eyes, distraction in's aspect.

ACT 2, SCENE 2.

One night when Henry Irving was playing Hamlet, he noticed an old lady in the front row of the pit dissolved in tears, and, delighted at this apparent appreciation of his acting, sent round word that he would like to see her after the performance.

"Madame," said Irving, "I perceived that my acting moved you very much."

"Indeed it did," she replied, still drying her eyes. "You see, I've a young son play-acting somewhere up north, and it broke me up to think that he might be no better at it than you!"

Tears seven times salt.

ACT 4, SCENE 5.

A Parisian happened to be present at Talma's performance of Hamlet, which, as usual, drew tears from nearly the whole of his audience.

Being questioned by a person sitting near him, who was astonished to perceive that he alone remained unaffected during the most pathetic scenes, the Parisian coolly replied, "I do not cry, because, in the first place, none of this is true; and secondly, if it was, what business is it of mine?"

Behind the Scenes - Diprose's Book of Stage and Players.

Prince Hamlet was a melancholy Dane
Who suffered from incipient insanity.
Existence was to him a perfect bane;
And life was but a humbug and a vanity.
He went about arrayed in garb of woe,
With funeral and gloomy physiognomy,
He preferred the works of Edgar Allan Poe
To volumes on political economy.

But he didn't love Ophelia as he "oughter",
Which sent Ophelia silly, so they say.
Said he, "Go find another,
I will love you as a brother."
But Ophelia wasn't built that way.

Anon.

Shards, flints and pebbles should be thrown on her.

ACT 5, SCENE 1.

Herbert Beerbohm Tree describing Mrs. Patrick Campbell's Ophelia:
"When she's good, she's divinely good; but when she's bad – Oh, my GOD!"

Now could I drink hot blood...
ACT 3, SCENE 2.

The actor, Hubert Carter, when he played Claudius, used to drink a pint of ox blood, fresh from the butcher's, every night before going on.

Richard Burton once drank a quart of brandy during his Broadway performance of Hamlet. The only visible signs being that he played the last two acts 'gay'.

It shall to the barber's, with your beard.
ACT 2, SCENE 2.

The tragedian T.C.King was famous for his heavy drooping moustache, which he could never be prevailed upon to remove. He also sported a very bushy pair of eyebrows, which unfortunately got burnt off one evening whilst studying Hamlet too close to a candle, so he had to substitute a realistic pair of wax ones instead; but, unfortunately, one night during the intense Closet Scene, theses melted off in a similar manner.

O, this is the poison of deep grief.
ACT 4, SCENE 5.

When asked for his impressions of William Poel's production with Esmé Percy, Henry James replied, "It was like morning prayers in the workhouse."

Hamlet rations out his situation by relieving himself in long soliloquy.
Student Bloopers. *Verbatim.* 1987.

O what a rogue and peasant slave am I!

ACT 2, SCENE 2.

The young actor Joe Cowen remembers witnessing Edmund Kean's *Hamlet of 1814.*

When Kean came on I was astonished. I was prepared to see a small man; but, diminished by the unusual distance and in his black dress, he appeared a perfect pigmy; his voice unlike any I had ever heard before, perhaps from its very strangeness, was most objectionable, and I at once pronounced him a most decided humbug; and if I could have got out then, I should have said so to everybody because I honestly thought so.

But I was obliged to remain, and compelled to be silent till it came to the dialogue with the ghost, and at the line, *I'll call thee Hamlet - King - father,* I was converted. I resigned the support of the lady, and employed both hands in paying the usual tribute to godlike talent. Father is not a pretty word to look at, but it is beautiful to hear when lisped by little children, or spoken by Edmund Kean in *Hamlet.*

Derek Jacobi as Kean, Haymarket Theatre 1990.

And let those that play your clowns speak no more than is set down for them.

ACT 3, SCENE 2.

TOMMY COOPER

To be, or not to be - that is the question:
Whether 'tis nobler in the mind to suffer
The slings and arrows of outrageous fortune…

(Turns to audience)

I had a bit of bad luck yesterday, I was pinched for parking. And, I said to the officer, I said, "Well I'm in a cul-de-sac." He said, "I don't care what kind of car it is, you can't park here."

(Back into Hamlet)

Or to take arms against a sea of troubles.

(Turns to audience)

I always travel by sea. I never fly. Well, I did once - I flew to America. And there was a film on board, and I'd already seen it, so I walked out half way through.

(Back into Hamlet)

And by opposing end them?
To die, to sleep -
To sleep perchance to dream.

(Turns to audience)

I had a funny dream last night. I dreamt I was eating a ten pound marsh mallow woke up this morning and found that the pillow was missing.

(Back into Hamlet)

With this regard their currents turn away
And lose the name of action. Soft you now,
The fair Ophelia.

(Turns to audience)

Now there's a girl for you. Pretty as a picture and not a bad frame either.

Part of a sketch from his *Life With Cooper* TV series.

To be, or not to be, that is the question...
ACT 3, SCENE 1.

Has there ever been a more boring speech,
after 400 years of constant repetition, than *To be or not to be?*
Richard Burton.

I confess myself utterly unable to appreciate that celebrated soliloquy and tell whether it be good, bad or indifferent. It has been handled and pawed about by declamatory boys and men, and torn so inhumanly from its living place and continuity in the play, till it has become to me a perfect dead number.
Charles Lamb.

Of course when you do that soliloquy everybody wants to join in. It's such an old number that they should have a song sheet.
Peter O'Toole.

The famous purple patch which everybody in the audience waits for.
John Gielgud.

James Quinn was once asked to audition a young gentleman who believed that he was born to be an actor. Hamlet's soliloquy was chosen, and when the young man had got as far as *To be, or not to be: that is the question*, Quinn interrupted him, in his booming voice, saying, "No question, sir, 'pon my honour - *not* to be, most certainly."

To be or not to be – and that's a question?
Milton Berle.

Good Hamlet cast thy nightly colour off...

ACT 1, SCENE 2.

Moody Dane,
Moody Dane,
Why are
You moody?
Broody Dane,
Broody Dane,
Don't be
So broody!
Smile a smile, dear,
Dry your eyes,
Try not to
Soliloquize.
Don't keep sayin':
"That's the question,"
It is only
Indigestion -
Moody Dane,
Moody Dane.
Don't be
So naughty!
It is all
Wrong to call
Your Momma
Bawdy -
There's a bend in every lane,
Soon the sun will shine again,
Skies of blue come after rain,
Moody Dane,
Moody Dane.

Herbert Farjeon. *Nine Sharp & Earlier.*

I shall not look upon his like again.

ACT 1. SCENE 2.

David Garrick *first played Hamlet at Drury Lane in December 1772 in a mutilated and slightly corrupt version of the original, leaving out 'All that would offend the ear.' He also cut out Osric the Grave-digger and the fencing scene between Hamlet and Laertes. His start of terror on seeing the Ghost became one of his great moments.*

Hamlet appears in black. Horatio and Marcellus are with him, in uniform; they are expecting the Ghost. Hamlet's arms are folded, and his hat overshadows his eyes: the theatre is darkened. Horatio, suddenly starts, exclaiming, *Look, my lord, it comes!* At these words Garrick turns suddenly about, at the same instant starting with trembling knees two or three steps backwards; his hat falls off; his arms, especially the left, are extended straight out, the left hand as high as his head, the right arm is more bent, and the hand lower, the fingers are spread far apart; and the mouth open; thus he stands, one foot far advanced before the other, in a graceful attitude, as if petrified, supported by his friends who fear that he will fall to the ground. His whole demeanour is so expressive of terror that it made my flesh creep even before he began to speak.

Georg Lichtenberg. 1775.

"I had sworn I would not leave the stage until I had rescued that noble play from the rubbish of the fifth act."
David Garrick.

*"Would not you, sir, start as Mr. Garrick
does if you saw a ghost?"
asked Boswell.*

*"I hope not,"
replied Dr. Johnson,
"for if I did, I believe I should frighten the ghost!"*

I swear I use no art at all.
ACT 2, SCENE 2.

Colonel Blimp's production at Poona.

Our Queen Gertrude, although suffering from several groups of adenoids, spoke up jolly well, which, I must say, helped considerably to get over the disappointment we had with our Ophelia. She was the bandmaster's wife and, unfortunately, was a trifle indisposed. However, realizing that there were no such things as actresses in Elizabeth's day, I ordered one of my buglers to play the part, and if it hadn't been that he refused to shave his moustache, I must say his rendering left nothing to be desired. In fact, during the mad scene, when he threw flowers about and said *There's rue for you* and all that, I don't think I ever saw anyone look quite so barmy in my life.

Seymour Hicks. *Hail Fellow Well Met.*

Her speech is nothing; yet the unshaped use of it doth move the hearers to collection.

ACT 4, SCENE 5.

When Glenda Jackson played Ophelia at Stratford in 1965, her mother and aunt both came up from Hoylake to see her and both reacted in quite different ways. After Ophelia's death, Mrs. Jackson dropped gently off to sleep whilst her aunt, convinced that her niece was really dead, stood up and started screaming.

Ophelia said I deplore
That young Hamlet's becoming a bore.
He just talks to himself,
I'll be left on the shelf -
Or dead by the end of Act Four.
Anon.

A truant disposition.

ACT 1, SCENE 2.

In the summer of 1787, at the Richmond Theatre, a certain Mr. Cubit was announced as Hamlet; a part which he was to act for the first time.

Just before the performance was going to begin Mr. Cubit was seized with a sudden and serious bout of terror, and fled the theatre.

Without a replacement and a house filled to capacity the play went on without the leading character - and was considered by the majority of the audience, Sir Walter Scott being one, to have been much improved.

In 1900 E.H.Sothern played a spectacular Hamlet at the Garden Theatre, New York, but the production was cancelled after less than a week when he was stabbed in the foot during sword play and contracted blood poisoning.

The humorous man shall end his part in peace.

ACT 2, SCENE 2.

George Robey *ruminates on how he would play Ophelia.*
Ophelia, poor wench, was too quiet. She let Hamlet have all his own way. If he made rude remarks, she never told him to *desist.* She just went dotty and drowned herself. Foolish fay! I hate those wet deaths.

If I ever play Ophelia I'll have a few good songs and dances written in to brighten things up a bit, so, whenever Hamlet comes butting in with his long-winded recitations, I will fetch him a swat across his refreshment department with my umbrella. Methinks that'll bring him to his knees, and *then* perhaps he will propose to me!

Ophelia ought to be a sure scream if it is played properly!
Sunday Chronicle. *Pantomime Annual,* 1912-13.

A hour of quiet shortly shall we see...

ACT 5, SCENE 2.

In 1896 a performance of *Hamlet* was given in dumb show with a certain Mr. Bellew reading the text from the front of the stage. An interesting idea if only the actors could have fitted in their gestures at the right moment to suit the speaker's words. By the end of the evening Mr. Bellew, at least two scenes ahead, took his applause and left the stage. The rest was silence.
Green Room Recollections. 1896.

What have I done that thou dar'st wag thy tongue In noise so rude against me?

ACT 3, SCENE 4.

Charles Macklin, a great tragedian and influential friend to Garrick, was famous for his long monumental pauses. On one occasion he paused so long that the prompter, thinking that his memory must have failed him, gave him his cue. Macklin rushed from the stage and knocked him down. "The fellow interrupted me in my Grand Pause," he explained to the audience, before continuing with the play.

I have words to speak... will make thee dumb.

Robert Helpmann *first performed the part in a ballet for Sadler's Wells at the New Theatre in 1942. The story is seen through the mind of the dying Hamlet and opens and closes on the same situation.*

Dear Mr. Helpmann,
I want you to know how very much I enjoyed your new ballet. As I have said many times to my husband, "Hamlet has been ruined by the words..."

O horrible, most horrible...

ACT 1, SCENE 4.

John Bannister *actor-manager, was greatly encouraged by Garrick to go on the stage, and describes in his memoirs his first highly unusual meeting with him.*

One morning I was shown into Garrick's dressing-room, where he was preparing to shave; a white night-cap covered his forehead; his chin and cheeks were enveloped in soap-suds and a razor-cloth was placed upon his left shoulder.

"Well, young man, so you are still for the stage, eh? What character do you - *should* you - like to - er... attempt?"

"I should like to attempt Hamlet, sir."

"Hamlet! What, Hamlet the Dane? Zounds, that's bold! Well, you'd better carry on and speak something. Don't worry about me shaving, I can hear you."

So, after a few hums and haws, I started.

Angels, and ministers of grace, defend us!
(he wiped his razor)
Be thou a spirit of health, or goblin damn'd
(he stropped the razor)
Bring with thee airs of heaven...
(he shaved his left side)
or blasts from hell
(he shaved his right)
Thou com'st in such a questionable shape...
Ouch! (he cut himself)
That I will speak to thee.
(he daubed the blood, and shaved on)
I call thee Hamlet, King, father, Royal Dane.
O, answer me!
(Silence.)

Then, to my eternal mortification, he turned quick upon me, brandishing the razor, and thrusting his half-shaved face close to mine, making such horrible mouths at me that I thought he was seized with insanity, exclaimed in a tone of ridicule *"Angels and ministers of grace, defend us!* Yaw, yaw, yaw, yaw!" He then put on his wig, took me by the hand, and with a smile of good nature began to act the speech himself; and how he spoke it, those who have heard him never can forget. "There, young sir, and when you perform that speech again, trying giving it more *passion* and less *mouth*."

Cleave the general ear with horrid speech…
ACT 2, SCENE 2.

Pip and his friend, Herbert Pocket, decide to see Mr. Wopsle appear as Hamlet.

On our arrival in Denmark, we found the King and Queen of that country elevated in two arm-chairs on a kitchen table, holding Court.

The late King of the country not only appeared to have been troubled with a cough at the time of his decease, but to have taken it with him to the tomb, and to have brought it back. The royal phantom also carried a ghostly manuscript round its truncheon, to which it had the appearance of occasionally referring, and that too, with an air of anxiety and a tendency to lose the place of reference which were suggestive of a state of mortality… The Queen of Denmark, a very buxom lady, though no doubt historically brazen, was considered by the public to have too much brass about her; her chin being attached to her diadem by a broad band of that metal (as if she had a gorgeous toothache), her waist being encircled by another, and each of her arms by another, so that she was openly mentioned as 'the kettledrum'. Lastly, Ophelia was a prey to such slow musical madness, that when, in course of time, she had taken off her white muslin scarf, folded it up, and buried it, a sulky man who had been long cooling his impatient nose against an iron bar in the front row of the gallery, growled, "Now the baby's put to bed, let's have supper!" Which, to say the least of it, was out of keeping.

Upon my unfortunate townsman, all these incidents accumulated with playful effect. Whenever that undecided Prince had to ask a question or state a doubt, the public helped him out with it. As for example; on the question whether *'Twas nobler in the mind to suffer*, some roared yes, and some no, and some inclining to both opinions said "Toss up for it"; and quite a Debating Society arose. When he asked what should some fellows as he do crawling between earth and heaven, he was encouraged with loud cries of "Hear, hear!" When he appeared with his stocking disordered (its disorder expressed, according to usage, by one very neat fold in the top, which I suppose to be always got up with a flat iron), a conversation took place in the gallery respecting the paleness of his leg, and whether it was occasioned by the turn the ghost had given him… When he recommended the player not to saw the air thus, the sulky man said, "And don't *you* do it, neither; you're a deal worse than *him*!" And I grieve to add that peals of laughter greeted Mr. Wopsle on every one of these occasions.

Charles Dickens. *Great Expectations.*

Revenge this foul and most unnatural murther.

ACT 1, SCENE 5.

When the R.S.C. performed Sherlock Holmes in the mid 70's, Punch magazine decided to give us their version of the meeting between the great Victorian detective and our favourite melancholy Dane.

ACT I
BAKER ST. No. 221B.
ENTER HAMLET.

HAM: Which one…
SHERL: …Of us is Holmes? 'Tis I. This gentle here
Is Watson, my devoted friend and colleague.
HAM: Good morrow to you both. You do not know me…
SHERL: Apart from knowing that you are a prince,
From Denmark, I would hazard, a solitary,
That you take snuff, have lately been at sea,
Were frightened by a horse at five and now
Are sitting for your portrait, you are a stranger.
WATS: Good heavens, Holmes!
HAM: Do you have magic powers?
SHERL: Sheer observation. You do wear a crown
And are a prince. You have a Danish accent,
Your shoes have late been knotted by a seaman,
There's snuff upon thy ruff, and on your doublet
Some Prussian Blue flicked by a careless painter.
HAM: All that you say is true, and yet I fear
You cannot guess my problem. To be brief,
My father was the King of Denmark, where
Now reigns his brother, my uncle, Claudius,
With as his wife my mother, the late Queen
And Queen again. Sir, I implore your aid.
What I seek to know
Is how my father was so cruelly murdered?
SHERL: Your father murdered? Are you sure of this?

HAM: Quite sure. My father's ghost has told me so.
SHERL: I see. (ASIDE) Quick Watson, get your gun. This man's
A raving lunatic. (TO HAMLET) You have a suspect?
HAM: I fear the foulest of my uncle, Claudius.
SHERL: No evidence?
HAM: Except that he poured poison
Into the ear of my poor sleeping father.
SHERL: How know'st thou this?
HAM: The ghost did tell me so.
SHERL: Hmm. (ASIDE) A talkative ghost.
(TO HAMLET) This case is not without its points of interest.
Within a day or so, sweet prince, I may well be
With you in Denmark.
HAM: My thanks. (EXITS)
SHERL: Or there again
I may well not. I've better things to do
Than listen to the babblings of mad youths.

Miles Kington. *Punch.*

Then up he rose, and donned his clothes...

ACT 4, SCENE 5.

Richmal Crompton *wrote a series of books following the hilarious exploits of Master William Brown. In William the Pirate, William is selected to take part in the school's Shakespeare competition, the chosen scene being from Hamlet. William immediately prepares himself, for he is sure to be offered the leading role, and indeed says as much to his girlfriend Dorinda. But much to his surprise the form master casts him as a humble attendant who stands throughout never saying a word. So as not to lose face with Dorinda, William learns Hamlet's big speech and on the day of the performance plans a special surprise.*

"Now don't forget," said the form master, who was also the producer, "you go on first of all and stand by the throne. Stand quite stiffly, as I showed you, and in a few moments the King and the others will come on." And William, his faculties still in a whirl, was thrust unceremoniously upon the empty stage.

He stood there facing a sea of upturned, intent faces. Among them in the second row he discerned that of Dorinda, her eyes fixed expectantly upon him.

Instinctively and without a moment's hesitatation, he stepped forward and with a sweeping gesture launched into his speech.

"To be, or not to be that is the question
Whether 'tis nobler in the mind to suffer -"...

"Come off, you young fool," hissed the form master wildly from behind the scenes.

But William had got well into his stride and was not coming off for anyone.

"The slings and arrows of outrageous fortune.
Or to take arms against a sea of troubles."

The best thing, of course would have been to lower the curtain, but there was no curtain to lower.

"Come *off*, I tell you," repeated the form master frantically.

"And by opposing end there. To sleep to die."

William had forgotten everything in the world but himself, his words, and Dorinda. He was unaware of the crowd of distraught players hissing and gesticulating off the stage; he was unaware of his form master's frenzied commands, of the frozen faces of the headmaster and Mr. Welbecker, who sat holding his shield ready for presentation in the front row.

"No more and by a sleep to say we end..."

William, vaguely aware that someone was trying to stop him saying his speech, reacted promptly, and dodged to the other side of the stage... Then followed the

diverting spectacle of the form master chasing William round the stage - William dodging, doubling, and all the time continuing his speech… A mighty roar ascended from the audience. Dorinda was rocking to and fro with mirth and clapping with all her might and main. The unseemly performance came to an end at last. The players joined the form master in the chase, and William, still reciting, was dragged ingloriously from the stage…

Dorinda was wiping tears of laughter from her eyes. "Wasn't William *wonderful?*" she said.

Richmal Crompton.

What, are they children? Who maintains 'em?

ACT 2, SCENE 2.

William Henry West Betty, the Young Roscius, took London by storm in the season of 1804-5, by playing Hamlet when he was only thirteen years of age - a part which he was reputed to have learnt in four days. Here is a contempory account of the frenzied scenes which occurred as patrons fought each other to gain the best seats.

Gentlemen, who knew there were no places untaken in the boxes and who could not get up the pit avenues, paid for admission into the lower boxes, and poured from them into the pit in 20's and 30's at a time. The ladies were occupied almost the whole night in fanning the gentlemen who were beneath them in the pit. Upwards of twenty gentlemen, who had fainted, were dragged up into the boxes. Several more raised their hands as if in the act of supplication for mercy and pity. Master Betty was not disturbed by the uproar of applause which welcomed him and answered the universal expectation.

This courtesy is not of the right breed.

ACT 3, SCENE 2.

When actors like William Charles Macready went on tour, they usually did so alone, and the towns that they played had to provide what support they could, professional or amateur or both.

During the rehearsals at a country theatre, Macready had occasion to find fault fairly frequently with a local actor who took the part of the King. The man was indignant at this constant criticism and apparently decided upon revenge, for, on the first night of the production, instead of remaining at the back of the stage when stabbed by Hamlet, he reeled to the centre and fell dead on the very spot that Macready had reserved for himself before he expired in Horatio's arms.

"Die further up the stage. What are you doing here? Get up and die elsewhere, sir," said the star under his breath. At this, to the amazement of the audience, the dead King sat up, and in a voice that could be heard all over the house said, "Look here, Mr. Macready, you've had your way at rehearsals; but I'm King now, and I shall die just where I please."

John Aye. *Humour in the Theatre.*

I'll rant as well as thou...
ACT 5, SCENE 1.

Whilst touring in Cincinnati in 1849 Macready was subjected to a great deal of audience hostility. These demonstrations were organised by the American actor Edwin Forrest, who was becoming envious of Macready's success.

Acted Hamlet to a rather rickety audience, but I tried my utmost, and engaged the attention of at least half the audience. In the scene after the play with Rosencrantz and Guildenstern, an occurrence took place that, for disgusting brutality, indecent outrage and malevolent barbarism, must be without parallel in the theatre of any civilised community.

Whilst speaking to them about 'the pipe', a ruffian from the left side gallery threw into the middle of the stage the half of the raw carcase of a sheep!

The paragon of animals.
ACT 2, SCENE 2.

A hapless stage manager recounts how he was forced to extend the repertoire of their resident dog act (which were all the rage at the time).

The proprietor sent for me and instructed me to change the bill. 'Give 'em some Shakespeare', he said. 'Put up *Hamlet.*'

I found our Dog-man and told him of the manager's suggestion. He was delighted with it. I enquired if he had ever played Hamlet. He replied, 'No, but that's all right. I'll wing it.' As Hamlet speaks considerably more than a thousand lines, this was a startling proposition. However, I called a rehearsal for the following morning. Our Dog-man came with a book of the play he had bought on his way to rehearsal. He separated the uncut leaves with a letter opener and began to read the part. Its length surprised him, and turning to me he remarked in a strong Cockney dialect, 'This bloomin' Dane don't 'alf cackle a lot.' He floundered through the first scene until he reached Hamlet's soliloquy beginning, 'Oh, that this too too solid flesh would melt,' etc. That was too much for him. He admitted defeat and departed abruptly, taking his dogs with him.

Frederick Warde. *Fifty Years of Make-Believe.*

In 1809, or thereabouts, at the Royal Circus in London, a performance of Hamlet was given by a troupe of dogs. There is no record, alas, whether or not the leading role was played by a Great Dane.

The cat will mew, and dog will have his day.

Act 5, Scene 1.

I was in the middle of *To be or not to.* Turning on *That is the question,* I found myself face to face with a black dog. The dog was looking at me critically, and I thought I might possibly edge him off the stage; and so I proceeded with the soliloquy, with one eye on the audience and one on the dog, punctuating my speech every now and again with a back kick at the enemy. Certainly the house was breathless with excitement. I backed the infernal animal into a corner, threw my mantle over it, got in a thundering kick and proceeded with my speech. My triumph was brief. To the delight of the audience the dog crawled out from under the mantle and charged ferociously in my direction. It evidently did not approve of me or my rendition of the text. The excitement rose to fever-heat. Suiting the action to the word - *with a bare bodkin* - I drew my sword, and with the flat of it warded off the animal's attack and, still reciting Shakespeare at my loudest, beat, pushed, and kicked the snarling creature into the prompt-corner. The flight of the prompt-corner's occupants attracted the animal to follow them off the stage and down the stairs, where someone put a fire bucket on its head and hurled it into the street.

Frank Benson. *My Memoirs.*

Hey non, nony, hey nony...

Act 4, Scene 5.

King George V, like his mother, was deaf, and was said to enjoy his playgoing chatting about racing with Sir Edward Elgar at the back of the box. Arriving for a charity matinée of *Hamlet* at the Haymarket Theatre one afternoon, Queen Mary asked the head of the Reception Committee what time the performance would be over. "You see," she said, "the King always has to have his tea punctually, and he is so anxious not to miss seeing the girl with straws in her hair."

John Gielgud. *Backward Glances.*

The stage can be defined as a place where Shakespeare murdered
Hamlet and a great many Hamlets have since murdered Shakespeare.
Robert Morse.

Take you me for a sponge, my lord?
ACT 4, SCENE 2.

How strange it is that I should have made the reputation I have as Hamlet with nothing to help me - with no equipment. My legs, my voice - everything has been against me. For an actor who can't walk, can't talk and has no face to speak of, I've done pretty well.

Henry Irving.

Irving's legs are distinctly *precious*, but his left leg is a *poem*.
Oscar Wilde.

O there be players that I have seen play...

ACT 3, SCENE 2.

Henry Irving was just reaching his 200th performance of Hamlet. Large posters decorated the ouside of the Lyceum Theatre announcing this "record" all over London. He was now at the very pinnacle of his success.

It chanced that Irving was standing in the Lyceum vestibule one afternoon, talking with his manager of this impending bi-centenary performance, when he noticed the famous actor Charles Dillon passing by. "Why, there's dear old Dillon!" he exclaimed, and dashed out to greet him.

"Ah, Mr. Dillon!" said Irving. "This is indeed a pleasure! It is years since we met. I hope you are well?"

"Sir!" thundered Dillon, "you have the advantage of me! Who are you, sir?"

"I am Henry Irving," gently responded the Lyceum star. "Surely you recall me, Mr. Dillon!

"No, sir!" growled Dillon. "I do *not* recall you! Nothing occurs to me concerning you - or your name!"

"I might perhaps remind you," quoth Irving, "that more than once I had the great privilege of playing Cassio - yes, even Cassio - to your grandly pathetic Othello. And I remember with great gratitude your kind words of encouragement, when you said to me: 'I regard you as showing a great deal of promise, Irving, my boy!'"

And then Dillon, in front of the very theatre placarded with posters of *"Henry Irving as Hamlet,"* retorted meditatively: "Irving? H'm, ye-es. Irving! I seem to remember the name... yes, yes. And so, what are you doing *now*, my boy?"

H.Chance Newton. *Cues and Curtain Calls.*

At the first Hamlet rehearsal, Irving followed his usual custom of reading the whole play aloud to his cast, indicating how he wanted each part acted.

The power that he put into each part was extraordinary. He threw himself so thoroughly into it that his skin contracted and his eyes shone. His lips grew whiter and whiter, and his skin more and more drawn as the time went on, until he looked like a livid thing, but beautiful.

Ellen Terry.

Looked upon his love with idle sight.
ACT 2, SCENE 2.

I went up to do "To be…" from the bowels of the stage one afternoon, and I could hear slight titter from the audience - I thought what are they laughing at? Anyway, I made some gesture or other to the face and discovered I was wearing my bloody horn-rimmed glasses. So I trudged through as far as I could, thinking of how to get get rid of them. And all I could think of was to sling them at Ophelia - "There will be no more marriages". And woomph, across the stage went flying lord Hamlet's prescription lenses!

Peter O'Toole.

Your leave and favour to return to France.

ACT 1, SCENE 2.

In 1899 Sarah Bernhardt *came to London with her controversial rendition of Hamlet.*
If it wasn't Hamlet it certainly was a tour de force on the part of the divine Sarah. I stood in the wings all the evening, and Shakespeare's verse in French fell strangely on the ear.

"Hélas! pauvre Yeorick, je connais bien, 'Oratio!"

I remember during the graveyard scene it was amusing to see the great actress turn her back to the audience and urge on the supers frantically, saying, *"Allez! allez! Vite - Vite!"* They were a gang of Cockneys in monks habits who hadn't the remotest idea what she meant.

Seymour Hicks. *Between Ourselves.*

One laugh in that dangerous atmosphere and the whole structure of polite solemnity would have toppled down, burying beneath its ruins the national reputation for good manners. I, therefore, like everybody else kept an iron control upon the corners of my lips. It was not until I was half way home and well out of earshot of the Adelphi that I unsealed the accumulations of my merriment.

Max Beerbohm.

After Bernhardt left London, she took her Hamlet to Stratford and then on to Edinburgh, where, because her costume failed to arrive in time, she played the part in a kilt.

What was I about to say?

ACT 2, SCENE 1.

Joss Ackland *in his autobiography remembers playing Claudius, in 1951, for the Salisbury Theatre Repertory Company . The rehearsal period was two weeks.*

Hamlet in two weeks was a big job for a young director. We were nowhere near ready when dress-rehearsal arrived, and it carried on through the night and the following day. When we opened to the public we were bleary-eyed and exhausted. So tired were we that when I made my first entrance as Claudius, to a fanfare of trumpets, I swept into the kneeling court, settled majestically on to a huge throne and said, *Though yet of -* and dried. During the long silence the court remained nervously on their knees but no prompt came to save me from the corner. Eventually someone backstage ran round and found the stage-manager, collapsed, fast asleep on the prompt book. Pushing him aside and hastily scanning the pages my saviour found the right place in the script. Placing one hand to his mouth he boomed out *Hamlet!...* I continued.

Joss Ackland. *I Must Be In There Somewhere.*

By the mass, I was about to say something.

ACT 2, SCENE 1.

The old tragedian was in his stride and pleasing the audience greatly until half way through Hamlet's advice to the players speech when his mind went blank. Nervously he scuttled to the prompt-corner.

"Yes?" he hissed.
"What?" asked the prompter.
"Where am I, you fool?"
"Page eighty-five."

'Tis gone and will not answer.

ACT 1, SCENE 1.

Frank Marshall (at the Marylebone Theatre, 1876), gave an intelligent reading of the unfortunate Prince. He also had one enormous advantage over the rest of the cast - *he* knew his part. The Ophelia was a lady who had never played in tragedy before, and when she did not quite catch the drift of Hamlet's well-intentioned efforts to assist her, sharply queried, *"What?"*

Arthur W.M. Beckett. *Green Room Recollections.*

In form and meaning how express and admirable.

ACT 2, SCENE 2.

Paul Scofield first played Hamlet in 1948 at Stratford in Michael Benthall's production, when he alternated the part with Robert Helpmann. Ken Tynan remembers his performance with great enthusiasm.

Unconvinced and tentative, he pads about the wide solitary stage, his turned-out feet going two ways in two minds, his tired hands flickering, his lips pursed and worried, inly hopeless and ever grasping joy. The matronly spectator may meditate adopting him as a pet, lean and shaggy in his hunger for solace. No sound he utters, no step he takes is fixed or purposed: there are no roots, he is a wandering plant, in sapless perambulation. Sometimes he will seem to make stern his lips with terrible earnestness; he will prowl around, inclined stiff-necked forwards, surveying the ground with the beady-eyed intentness of a schoolmistress rolling up her sleeves to investigate an evil smell in the changing-room; but always the fraily shrugging hands contradict his designs. Nothing he does is confidently predictable. Even the simplest move over the stage may be dammed and diverted by some new roaming of his vague, merciful eyes. He commands all the silent agonies of childhood; in him the gravity of extreme youth and the puckishness of old age commingle. To have these qualities, and yet resolutely repel any hint of pathos, is one negative mark of great acting.

This is the best Hamlet I have seen… I know that there is now in England a young actor who is bond-slave to greatness.

Kenneth Tynan. *He That Plays The King.*

Look here upon this picture, and on this…

Act 3, Scene 4.

Jonathan Pryce played both Hamlet and the Ghost at the Royal Court Theatre, April 1980.
Jill Bennett played his mother.

The insolence of office...
ACT 3, SCENE 1.

Two of the supporting cast in Burton's Hamlet were supposed to lower a flag over the Prince during his dying speech. The flag was lowered, the house hushed. And as the dark and tragic Hamlet uttered his last words, one of these rather camp gentleman murmured out of the side of his mouth; "So, who's the boy in black then?"

Michael Benthall, the director, was very keen, during this particular production, to have more ensemble playing during the Play Scene - and asked everyone to think of an ad lib or two to help build the dramatic impact on the King's exit. Which dutifully they did. In the midst of the confusion, during one performance, an actor's voice could be heard above the rest - "Thanks Prince for a lovely party!"

Give me your pardon, sir. I've done you wrong.
ACT 5, SCENE 2.

Junius Brutus Booth once took great pity on a horse thief from Louisville called Lovett, providing him with a lawyer. But the thief was found guilty and sentenced to be hanged. To thank him for all that he had done Lovett bequeathed his head to Booth, with the request that "he would use it on the stage when playing Hamlet, and think when he held it in his hands of the gratitude his kindness had awakened." In 1857 it was sent to Edwin Booth, the son of Junius, who on several occasions used it in the grave-yard scene in *Hamlet*, and finally had it buried.

Incidentally, Junius in later life used to suffer from bouts of uncontrollable madness. Once during the Play Scene he turned on a shocked Boston audience and yelled "I'm insane, I tell you. Take me to an asylum!"

> **W**e sit before the row of evening lamps,
> Each in his chair,
> Forgetful of November dusks and damps,
>   And wintry air.
>
> And, beautiful as dreams of maidenhood
> That doubt defy,
> Young Hamlet, with his forehead grief-subdued,
>   And visioning eye.

Julia Ward Howe on Edwin Booth's Hamlet.

ON, SATURDAY, MAY 14, 1793, BY HIS MAJESTY'S COMPANY OF COMEDIANS.
(The last night, because the Company go to-morrow to Waterford.)
Will be performed, by command of several respectable people in this learned
metropolis, for the benefit of Mr. KEARNS

THE TRAGEDY OF HAMLET

Originally written and composed by the celebrated
Dan Hayes of Limerick, and inserted in Shakespeare's works.

HAMLET BY MR. KEARNS,

(being his first appearance in that character,) who, between the acts, will perform
several solos on the patent bagpipes, which play two tunes at the same time.

OPHELIA BY MRS. PRIOR,

who will introduce several favourite airs in character particularly
"The Lass of Richmond Hill," and **"We'll all be unhappy together,"**
from the reverend Mr. Dibdin's Oddities.

The parts of the King and Queen, *by direction of the* Rev. Father O'Callaghan,
will be omitted, as too immoral for any stage.

Polonius, the comical politician, by a young gentleman,
being his first appearance in public.

The Ghost, The Grave digger, and Laertes, by Mr. Sampson,
the great London comedian. The characters to be dressed in Roman shapes.

To which will be added, an Interlude, in which will be introduced several
slight-of-hand tricks, by the celebrated surveyor Hurt.

To conclude with the Farce of
MAHOMET THE IMPOSTOR
Mahomet by Mr. Kearns.
Tickets to be had of Mr. Kearns at the sign of the Goat's Beard, in Castle Street.
The value of the tickets, as usual will be taken, in candles, bacon, soap, butter, &c.
as Mr. Kearns wishes, in every particular, to accommodate his public.

N.B. - No person whatsoever will be admitted into the boxes without shoes or stockings.

Be not too tame neither...
ACT 3, SCENE 2.

Noël Coward went to see Leslie Howard's Hamlet in America and found his whole performance muted and impassive. At the end he went round to Howard's dressing room and embraced him, saying, "Oh, Leslie, you know how I hate over-acting - and you, darling boy, could never, ever over-act - but please on this one occasion, *do try.*"

What roars so loud and thunders in the index?
ACT 3, SCENE 4.

Macready growls and prowls, and roams and foams, about the stage, in every direction, like a tiger in his cage, so that I never know on what side of me he means to be; and keeps up a perpetual snarling and grumbling, so that I never feel quite sure that he has done, and that it is my turn to speak.

Fanny Kemble.

No more like my father than I to Hercules.
ACT 1, SCENE 2.

One evening while Charles Mayne Young was playing Hamlet at the Haymarket, he was severely and persistently hissed from one corner of the theatre. He soon succeeded in detecting the malevolent personage, and recognised in him his own father. Not the first time that this excellent gentleman had given public proof of animosity against his children.

Hamlet is a hoop through which every eminent actor must, sooner or later, jump.

Max Beerbohm.

What's Hecuba to him, or he to Hecuba,
That he should weep for her?

ACT 2, SCENE 2.

Fanny Kemble describes playing Ophelia opposite her father, Charles Kemble.

I have acted Ophelia three times with my father, and each time, in that beautiful scene where his madness and his love gush forth together like a torrent swollen with storms, that bears a thousand blossoms on its troubled waters, I have experienced such deep emotion as hardly to be able to speak. The exquisite tenderness of his voice, the wild compassion and forlorn pity of his looks, bestowing that on others which, of all others, he most needed; every shadow of expression and intonation was so full of the mingled anguish that the human heart is capable of enduring, that my eyes scarce fixed on his ere they were filled with tears; and long before the scene was over, the letters and jewel-cases I was tendering to him were wet with them.

What's Hecuba to him? Mere fancy! Piffle!
Yet I, poor wight, can't muster up a sniffle.
Marry, come up! My conduct is surprising.
To walk about like this, soliloquizing.
**From *The Flea* - a scurrilous and amusing paper, published by
members of Frank Benson's company.**

I'll not be juggled with.

ACT 4, SCENE 5.

The Prince of Denmark isn't a man with whom I would like to spend a weekend.
Hamlet talked far too much and did too little.
R.C.Sherriff.

The Tragedy of *Hamlet* is a coarse and barbarous piece, which would not be tolerated by the basest rabble in France or Italy - one would think that this work was the fruit of the imagination of a drunken savage.
Voltaire.

It harrows me with fear and wonder.

ACT 1, SCENE 1.

In his novel Tom Jones, Henry Fielding describes the effect that David Garrick's perform-ance has on the naive Mr Partridge, who has never seen the play or heard of the great actor, and on his friend, Mr Jones.

As soon as the play, which was *Hamlet, Prince of Denmark*, began, Partridge was all attention, nor did he break silence till the entrance of the ghost; upon which he asked Jones, "What man that was in the strange dress... Sure it is not armour, is it?" Jones answered, "That is the ghost." To which Partridge replied with a smile, "Persuade me to that, sir, if you can. Though I can't say I actually saw a ghost in my life, yet I am certain I should know one, if I saw him, better than that comes to. No, no, sir, ghosts don't appear in such dresses as that, neither." In this mistake, which caused much laughter in the neighbourhood of Partridge, he was suffered to continue, 'til the scene between the ghost and Hamlet, when Partridge fell into so violent a trembling, that his knees knocked against each other. Jones asked him what was the matter, and whether he was afraid of the warrior upon the stage?

"O la! sir," said he, "I perceive now it is what you told me. I am not afraid of anything; for I know it is but a play: and if it was really a ghost, it could do no harm at such a distance, and in so much company; and yet if I was frightened, I am not the only person."

"Why, who," cries Jones, "dost thou take to be such a coward here besides thyself?" "Nay, you may call me a coward if you will; but if that little man there upon that stage is not frightened, I never saw any man frightened in my life... Oh! here is again. - *No farther!* No, you have gone far enough already; farther than all the King's dominions." Jones offered to speak, but Partridge cried, "Hush, hush, dear sir, don't you hear him!" And during the whole speech of the ghost, he sat with his eyes fixed partly on the ghost, and partly on Hamlet, and with his mouth open; the same passions which succeeded each other in Hamlet, succeeded likewise in him.

Henry Fielding.

Dear God, send me a good Hamlet - but make him cheap.
Lilian Baylis.

*Nay then, let the devil wear black, for
I'll have a suit of sables.*

One night during his last acting years, when called to the second act in *Hamlet*, Frank Benson suddenly asked: "What's the play?" "*Hamlet*, sir," said the shocked call-boy. "Ah, yes," said Benson, glancing down at his own costume, "Sables - I might have known."

The glass of fashion...
ACT 3, SCENE 1.

Henry Irving's Hamlet also had the immense advantage of the performance of Ellen Terry *as Ophelia. This was her first appearance at the Lyceum, and she planned to use her understanding of costume to her own advantage and discussed her ideas with Irving.*

"In the first scene I wear a pinkish dress. It's all rose-coloured with her. Her father and her brother love her. The Prince loves her - and so she wears pink."

"Pink," repeated Henry, thoughtfully.

"In the nunnery scene I have a pale, gold, amber dress... and in the last scene I wear a transparent, black dress."

Henry did not wag an eyelid. "I see. In mourning for her father."

"No, not exactly that. I think *red* was the mourning colour of the period. But black seems to me *right* - like the character, like the situation."

"Would you put the dresses on?" said Henry, gravely.

At that minute Walter Lacy came up, that very Walter Lacy who had been with Charles Kean when I was a child, and who now acted as advisor to Henry Irving in his Shakespearean productions.

"Ah, here's Lacy. Would you mind, Miss Terry, telling Mr. Lacy what you are going to wear?"

Rather surprised, but still unsuspecting, I told Lacy all over again. Pink in the first scene, yellow in the second, black -

You should have seen Lacy's face at the word 'black'. He was going to burst out, but Henry stopped him. He was more diplomatic than that!

"Ophelias generally wear *white*, don't they?"

"I believe so," I answered, "but black is more interesting."

"I should have thought you would look much better in white."

"Oh, no!" I said.

And then they dropped the subject for that day. It *was* clever of him!

The next day Lacy came up to me:

"You didn't really mean that you are going to wear black in the mad scene?"

"Yes, I did. Why not?"

"*Why not!* My God! Madame, there must be only one black figure in this play, and that's Hamlet!"

Ellen Terry. *The Story of My Life.*

Until my eyelids will no longer wag.

Herbert Beerbohm Tree *became manager of the Haymarket Theatre in 1887 where his only great resounding failure was his Hamlet of 1892. Max Beerbohm (Tree's half-brother) reluctantly accompanied some friends to a performance of this notorious production.*

During the evening his hosts looked around to find his chair unoccupied, but soon found him curled up on a pile of overcoats in the passage, dozing. He woke and murmured apologetically, "I am so sorry. I always enjoy Herbert's Hamlet this way."
John Gielgud.

Do you know how they are going to decide the Shakespeare-Bacon dispute? They are going to dig up Shakespeare and Bacon and then set their coffins side by side. They are then going to invite Beerbohm Tree to recite Hamlet to them. The one who turns in his coffin first, will be the rightful author of the play!
W.S.Gilbert

You will burst your waistcoat buttons,
Though sewn tightly on they be,
If you chance to see the Hamlet
Of our only Beerbohm Tree.
P.G. Wodehouse.

Dost thou know this waterfly?

ACT 5, SCENE 2.

My dear fellow, I never saw anything so funny in my life,
and yet it was not in the least bit vulgar.
W.S.Gilbert after witnessing Tree's Hamlet.

When sorrows come, they come not single spies, But in battalions.

ACT 4, SCENE 5.

Mrs. Mountford was an actress of considerable fame. After her retirement from the stage, love and the ingratitude of a bosom friend deprived her of her senses, and she was placed in a receptacle for lunatics. One day, during a lucid interval, she asked her attendant what play was to be performed that evening, and was told it was *Hamlet*. Whilst on the stage, she had been received with rapture as Ophelia. The recollection struck her and with the cunning which is so often allied to insanity she eluded the care of the keepers and got to the theatre. There she concealed herself until the scene in which Ophelia enters in her insane state; she then pushed herself onto the stage and exhibited a more perfect representation of madness than the utmost exertions of mimic art could effect; she was in truth Ophelia herself, to the amazement of the performers and astonishment of the audience.

Nature having made his last effort, her vital powers failed her. On going off, she exclaimed, *"It is all over!"* She was immediately conveyed back to her place of security, and a few days after, like a lily drooping, she hung her head, and died.

Richard Ryan. *Dramatic Table Talk.*

Loved of the distracted multitude...

ACT 4, SCENE 2.

I have seen 27 different Hamlets and none can touch Gielgud's - for me the definitive interpretation. One evening at dinner I asked him a stupid and unnecessary question: "What are the most essential things about acting?" With hardly a pause John replied: "Feeling and timing," then with his head erect, his eyes twinkling to one side (a favourite expression of his), he added, "I understand it is the same in many walks of life." I have seen him use the same expression as Hamlet when, facing the front, he said:

...Give me that man
That is not passion's slave, and I will wear him
In my heart's core, ay, in my heart of hearts
(*a pause, his eyes only turn to Horatio*)
As I do thee.
Donald Sinden.

But beshrew my jealousy!
ACT 2, SCENE 1.

John Gielgud once said to Peggy Ashcroft: "I don't really know what jealousy is. Oh yes, I do! When Larry had a success as Hamlet, I wept."

When Olivier played Hamlet in 1937, Gielgud went back-stage and said: "Larry, it's one of the finest performances I have ever seen, but it's still my part."

Now my Lord, you played once i' th' university, you say?

ACT 3, SCENE 2.

Emlyn Williams *remembers the occasion when, in 1924, he was asked at the eleventh hour to take over the prompt book at the Oxford University Dramatic Society's production of* Hamlet.

It was as if I had been offered a leading part which I already knew: there was all the excitement and none of the apprehension. A sandwich in the J.C.R. - "hello Byam Shaw, odd time to be eating but I'm due at the New stage door, bit of a crisis!" - and I hurried off, past the lighted front of the theatre, to the little long-forbidden door. I found myself straight on the stage, in the shadow of a great cyclorama and under a glaring working light; workmen hammering, stagehands sweeping, young men in shirt-sleeves and plus-fours dusting cardboard goblets. I hung my gown on a nail and tiptoed to the stool in the prompt-corner, getting up when Lockhart-Smith the stage-manager hurried down - shirt sleeves, plus-fours - with a Temple Shakespeare, "Christ, it hasn't got the cuts"… When people ran up to him he was 'Ken' to them all, but as sternly composed as a sea-captain of fifty, "There's an extra gelatine on the o.p. side, but tell Bobbie or Greville to pop over to the club and ask J.B. first." The Christian names scattered like sparks, "Reggie, have you tested the warning light under the stage - and Frank, check that the Ophelia mad wig is back and tell Bert I want a word with him about that bloody awful make-up he put on Patrick, J.B. said it turned Osric into something out of the Insect Play." Then, to me, "Williams - is that right - the one thing, Williams, you must do as a prompter is - *don't prompt*, unless there's a dead emergency, which you'll soon spot if you've done some acting, Willie says you have."

He left me with my Temple; by craning I could see into the wings, otherwise my view was of three-quarters of the acting area. Lights were being turned off; the soft tread of many people passing upstage, whispered good-lucks in the shadows. My corner was two feet from the red plush curtain at which I had stared longingly from the pit, and I could hear the audience drifting in; as the activity near me simmered to orderly twilight, so out there the murmur feverishly grew. Suddenly there was the orchestra - playing Byrd, I found later - and our side of the curtain was a lilting pool of confident promise. Applause; then I guessed, from the multiple chatter swiftly fading out into silence, that the house-lights had dimmed. The curtain still down, the lights on stage came up slow and sure on the haunted battlements. Miles away in the Elsinore air, a great bell boomed the ominous twelve of midnight; then, two feet from me, with an imperious sweep, the curtain rose. From the upper darkness, a voice. "Who's there?"

The first sight of Hamlet seated apart, six feet from me, black of hair and dress and mien, took my prompting breath away, so it was as well that he knew lines which he spoke with moving simplicity. The scene with the Ghost, green-armoured and thrillingly resonant, ending on the steps in a slow icy dawn over the battlements, grew on me with each performance. Tirelessly I studied the professional Gertrude and Ophelia, and although I was for the whole week under a spell, I never missed one effect they made, one move or one pause, and every time waited for each one so as to mark its apparent spontaneity - as on "Get thee to a nunnery," when Ophelia turned, unbelieving, and slowly put her hands to her face… I was learning. The spell worked all-powerfully, because what I experienced was unique: not having attended one rehearsal, and not once - through five nights and three matinées - seeing one actor out of make-up and costume, I stayed under a continuous illusion and yet an integral part of that illusion… Outside the theatre, I lived a shadow among shadows, for the only students I knew were from Wittenberg: my room a chimera, my bed a kip between one Elsinore and the next. It was only when I sank into my corner and heard the orchestra climb to "House Out", that the people I knew - Bernardo, Francisco - swam into flesh-and-blood focus.

Life began, for me, on the stroke of stage midnight. Wednesday, one p.m., sitting in the J.C.R. with coffee, sandwich and *Daily Mail* - "he was a boyish Hamlet" - I looked round at two blazered men accoutred for the river and thought, if only I could wear something that told the world I have a matinée! A pair of gold-laced Greek buskins? A make-up towel negligently round the neck? I looked at the clock and left for Denmark.

Emlyn Williams. *George*.

How is it that the clouds still hang on you?
ACT 1, SCENE 2.

This evening I am engaged to spend with a foreigner. He is a Dane, unjustly deprived of his father's fortune by his mother's marrying a second time. I have never yet seen him, but I hear that all the world will be there, which I think is a little unfeeling, as he is a little low-spirited sometimes almost to madness. For my part, from what I have heard, I do not think the poor young man will live out the night.

Hannah Moore, in a letter to her family, 1776.

A fellow of infinite jest, of most excellent fancy.

ACT 5, SCENE 1.

John Barrymore, *electrified New York in 1922 with his Hamlet, which ran for a record of 101 performances. Members of the Players Club were upset because he had not stopped at 99 in respect for Edwin Booth's record 100 performances. He returned to the role in 1925 at London's Haymarket Theatre.*

During the famous *O, what a rogue and peasant slave am I,* Barrymore painfully eased his body, which was exhausted from a full day of alcohol and "whoopee", onto a three-foot wall, held his dizzy head in his hands, and dangled his legs to keep the blood running. He chose this new piece of staging, he said, not out of spirit of invention but because he feared that any further moments on his feet would make him vomit! Later in the performance, he actually darted off the stage to throw up in the wings.

On the following morning, he received even better notices for his performance than he had in New York. Some London reviewers commented on the "brilliant leg-dangling"; "The face in the hands"; "The sudden rushing off, only to return immediately - his face ashen."

The croaking raven doth bellow for revenge.

ACT 3, SCENE 2.

Barrymore had a furious temper when it came to audience interruption, especially coughing. One evening when a chronic bout of bronchial hysteria was constantly smothering his lines, Barrymore came on for the second act and reaching inside his coat, produced a large fish. "Here, you damned walruses, busy yourself with that while we *try* and go on with the rest of the play."

He was once driven to distraction by the endless clinking of matinée tea-trays. It was so loud that he stopped in the middle of a soliloquy and turned in fury upon his elderly audience shouting "Tea-tea-tea! Is that all you English are interested in?"

His pranks have been too broad to bear with.

ACT 3, SCENE 4.

During rehearsals for *Hamlet*, John Barrymore hired a number of walk-ons to carry Ophelia's body to the grave. He stopped the first run-through and urged them to look less like chorus-girls and more like virgins.

"My dear Mr. Barrymore," retorted one of the ladies, "we are extras, not character actresses."

Ay, there's the rub.

ACT 3, SCENE 1.

While my father [Cedric Hardwicke] was playing at the Birmingham Rep in the 1920's, Bransby Williams presented his touring production of *Hamlet* for a week, and a group of young Rep actors, including my dad, went to see it. They were amazed to find that the evening started with *To be or not to be...* which normally doesn't appear till Act 3, Scene 1. Afterwards they managed to get to see Bransby Williams and politely asked him why he had done this. "Well," he explained, "after Hamlet had seen the Ghost, how could he possibly say *The bourne from which no traveller returns* – he couldn't now, could he?"

Edward Hardwicke.

Has this fellow no feeling of his business?

ACT 5, SCENE 1.

I have heard Frank Benson tell a story of how, on one occasion, no property coffin being available, a grandfather's clock, covered with a pall, was brought on instead, and in the middle of Hamlet's speech it started striking.

Elizabeth Fagin. *From the Wings.*

I have been in continual practice.

ACT 5, SCENE 2.

Sir Frank Benson was also an all-round athlete with a passion for cricket. According to Seymour Hicks, Sir Frank's contracts with his artists were always worded: "To play the Ghost in *Hamlet* and keep wicket, and also a fast bowler to play Laertes.**"** When he received a wire back informing him that a fast bowler was possible, but whether he could play Laertes remained to be seen, Benson replied; "Any fast bowler can play Laertes - any *good* fast bowler that is."

It was also said that no Polonius need apply unless he happened to be a first-class wicket-keeper.

What, has this thing appeared again tonight?
ACT 5, SCENE 2.

*Ralph Michael remembers playing Horatio to the Hamlets of Robert Speaight
and Robert Harris at the Old Vic in 1930.*

By the time we got to *Hamlet*, 'Bobby' Speaight was sharing the part with Robert
Harris, and I was playing Horatio to both of them.

Came the night of exposure. The moment of truth. Speaight was fighting Richard
Ainley, who played Laertes. As Hamlet lunged, the seam of his breeches, where fly-
buttons might have been, split open wide, causing his little 'member' to pop in and out.
Unaware of this, the Prince of Denmark duelled on, eventually dying, with his legs wide
open, upon the throne! I delicately dropped his leather waist-coat over the offending
embarrassment as I said, "Now cracks a noble heart. Good-night, sweet Prince, and
flights of angels sing thee to thy rest!"

Enter Fortinbras, with the memorable line, "Where is this sight?"

From that moment till the final curtain, there was deep silence, no applause only the
muffled laughter from the wings where the stage-hands, convulsed with glee, lay
prostrate in each others arms.

Ralph Michael.

When young Hamlet played the fool
His mood was quite euphoric.
He'd tease his mother as a rule
Or dig up bits of Yorick.

Instant Sunshine.

Chocolates.

Here are the seats; George, old man,
Get some chocolates while you can.

Quick the curtain's going to rise,
(Either Cadbury's or Spry's)

"The castle ramparts, Elsinore"
(That's not sufficient, get some more)

There's the *Ghost*; he does look wan
(Help yourself, and pass them on)

Doesn't *Hamlet* do it well?
(This one is a caramel)

Polonius's beard is fine
(Don't you grab; that big one's mine)

Look the *King* can't bear the play
(Throw that squashy one away)

Now the *King* is at his prayers
(Splendid, there are two more layers)

Hamlet's going for his mother
(Come on, Tony, have another)

Poor *Ophelia*! Look, she's mad
(However many's Betty had?)

The *Queen* is dead and so's the *King*
(Keep that lovely silver string)

Now even *Hamlet* can no more
(Pig! You've dropped it on the floor)

That last Act's simply full of shocks
(There's several left, so bring the box)
Guy Boas. *Punch, 1925.*

This same skull, sir, was Yorick's skull, the King's jester.

ACT 5, SCENE 1.

The first night in the West End gave the stage management some alarming moments. The scene in the churchyard was played on a platform. Below this was the real stage, which served as the bottom of the grave. Here the skulls were carefully placed. It seemed to me, when I walked on with Horatio, that an air of thoughtfulness, one might have said of strain, hung over the First Grave-Digger. I suddenly saw what had happened a few lines before we came to the best part of the scene. The skull was missing. And soon I must begin the *Alas, poor Yorick* speech, holding it in my hands. Should I orate over an imaginary skull? I dared not hope that the audience's imagination would follow me so far. I suddenly decided to cut out thirty lines. I jumped to *But soft, but soft awhile - here comes the king,* the words which introduce Ophelia's funeral procession, which was fortunately forming in the wings at that very moment. There was a short pause while the surprised mourners hurried to their places, then the procession entered. I learned afterwards that owing to the rake of the stage the skulls had rolled out of the grave-digger's reach. There was nothing to be done, though the distracted stage manager had tried, without avail, to borrow another skull from the Globe Theatre next door, where Alexander Moissi was playing Hamlet in a German version.

John Gielgud. *Early Stages.*

We have many pocky corses nowadays...

ACT 5, SCENE 1.

There's an apocryphal story about Andrew Leigh, the former Old Vic director, who bequeathed his skull to the theatre, at the Equity minimum salary; then about £3 a week!

When Macready played Hamlet in Baltimore they gave him a skull "of a negro who was hung two years ago for cutting down his overseer!"

In 1755, a critic objected to real skulls and bones in the grave-yard scene and suggested a wooden substitute be made by a carpenter. To meet such susceptibilities in Scotland, a grave-digger handed Hamlet "a small, consumptive and rather grimy turnip," instead.

This skull had a tongue in it, and could sing once.

ACT 5, SCENE 1.

George Frederick Cooke, *who excelled so greatly in other characters but failed, miserably, in Hamlet, is probably the only actor to have appeared on the stage after his death. When he died in New York, an American friend of his called Dr. Francis, somehow managed to get hold of Cooke's skull as a memento.*

A theatrical benefit had been announced at the Park, and *Hamlet* the play. A subordinate of the theatre hurried at a late hour to my office, for a skull. I was compelled to loan them the head of my old friend, George Frederick Cooke. Alas, poor Yorick!

Ken Dodd as Yorick in Kenneth Branagh's film of *Hamlet*.

This grave shall have a living monument.
ACT 5, SCENE 2.

In the spring of 1931, Donald Wolfit toured extensively for Charles Doran's company. One night at Newport the scenery only arrived at short notice and was hurriedly thrown under the stage without due examination.

That night the play was *Hamlet* and the stage-manager rushed at me during the evening exclaiming that Ophelia's coffin was under the stage and must be brought up for the graveyard scene. Together with a stage-hand and the carpenter we unearthed the long grey oblong from beneath a pile of props just in time to place it on the bier and cover it with a large purple pall. In the action of the scene this object was duly carried on, and as the second grave-digger it was my duty to take one end of it and lower it into the grave-trap. The purple pall having been lifted, there lay the box and uppermost, facing Claudius and the tragic Queen Gertrude who stood above the grave, was a large printed label: *Pickfords. Not wanted on the voyage.*

Donald Wolfit. *First Interval.*

Lady, shall I lie in your lap?
ACT 3, SCENE 2.

A famous Shakespearean actor was once approached by a young lady and asked if he felt it was true that Hamlet went to bed with Ophelia. "Well, I'm not sure what Shakespeare intended," said the actor. "But I usually do."

Prince Hamlet thought Uncle a traitor
For having it off with his Mater;
Revenge Dad or not ?
That's the gist of the plot,
And he did - nine soliloquies later.
Stanley J. Sharpless.

Then weigh what loss your honour may sustain...

ACT 1, SCENE 3.

Anthony Quayle played Laertes opposite Alec Guinness's *Hamlet, Cairo, 1939.*

On the opening night of *Hamlet* in Cairo, I fell through the stage - at least I fell through the rostrum that had been dropped in the Tagus. I came running on, sword in hand, shouting, *Where is this King? Sirs, stand you all without.* There was a cracking noise, and I fell through the rotted planks and disappeared from sight.

I was not hurt, but I was entombed in a dusty wooden cave. First I threw out my sword which was greeted by the audience with applause and a storm of laughter; then I jumped up and scrambled out myself.

All the time I had been shouting *O, thou vile King - give me my father -* to which the king (Andrew Cruickshank) had only one, inopportune, line in reply: *Calmly good Laertes.* This only increased the hilarity of the audience. By the time I emerged, both Andrew and the Queen (Cathleen Nesbitt) had given up all attempt to act; they had turned their backs to the audience with tears of laughter running down their faces.

Order was eventually restored, but Alec's Graveyard Scene and the whole ending of the play were wrecked. Alec was not pleased to have his opening night in Cairo so ruined, but he was generous and had forgiven me by the next day.

Anthony Quayle. *A Time to Speak.*

Since brevity is the soul of wit...

ACT 2, SCENE 2.

Richard Briers last night played Hamlet like a demented typewriter.
W.A.Darlington. *Daily Telegraph. 1954.*

The Reduced Shakespeare Company holds the world record for the fastest performance of *Hamlet*, at 42.2 seconds. In 1975, an East German company performed the play in 18 seconds but the record was disallowed after their Ophelia tested positive for steroids.

His beard was grizzly, no?

ACT 1, SCENE 2.

Alec Guinness was twenty-four when he first appeared as Hamlet in Tyrone Guthrie's modern dress production at the Old Vic, in 1938. In 1951, he was given carte blanche to put together something spectacular for the Festival of Britain, and again he chose Hamlet - the result being an unmitigated disaster.

Alec Guinness is a thinker as well as an actor - a fusion encountered as seldom as Halley's Comet. After much consideration, he decided to play the Dane with a beard. He won't do it again. Had David Garrick or Sir Henry Irving or Beerbohm Tree profaned Hamlet with whiskers? No! Then let's have no more of such hanky-panky.

Tallulah Bankhead.

Alec Guinness as Hamlet. New Theatre. 1951.

You jig, you amble and you lisp...
ACT 3, SCENE 1.

Guinness's first Shakespearean role was as Osric in Gielgud's production at the New in 1934, despite the fact that J.G. seemed to keep firing him during rehearsals.

It was after a week of rehearsing Hamlet that he spoke 'spontaneously' to me, with shattering effect. *"What's happened to you?"* he cried. *"I* thought you were rather good. You're terrible. Oh, go away! I don't want to see you again!"

I hung around at rehearsals until the end of the day and then I approached him cautiously. "Excuse me, Mr. Gielgud, but am I fired?"

"No! Yes! No, of course not. But go away. Come back in a week. Get someone to teach you how to act."

I mooched around for a week, mostly walking in London parks, and then, heart in mouth, reported back for rehearsals in St. Martin's Lane.

He seemed pleased to see me, heaped praise on my Osric and laughed delightedly at the personality (very water-fly) which I had assumed. I could swear I wasn't doing anything different from what I had done before but, suddenly and briefly, I was teacher's pet. "Motleys! Motleys, you should give him a hat with a lot of feathers, like the Duchess of Devonshire!"

Alec Guinness.

I must be cruel, only to be kind.
ACT 3, SCENE 4.

Part of a review from the Indianapolis Herald of 1875 for Barry Sullivan's Hamlet. A certain Harry Dalton was giving his Horatio.

What can we say of Mr. Dalton? It is our duty to scalp him, that's plain; but shall we do so gingerly, or with a whoop and a bold flourish of the knife? Look here, Mr. Dalton, you were not designed for the stage, but if you are to remain upon it then in Heaven's name do something to keep your hands to yourself, and break off the habit of reaching out in that style so suggestive of "Simon says wiggle-wiggle! Simon says thumbs up!" Put them in your ears; tie them across the small of your back; shove them into your boot-tops; get them out of sight whatever you do. They haunt us hideously. You are also guilty of squinting and winking your eyes. Pray you avoid this. And when you open your mouth to speak, try and keep from saying more than one word at once. That's all.

Robert Sillard. *Barry Sullivan and His Contemporaries.*

Let your own discretion be your tutor...

ACT 3, SCENE 2.

When the college society decided to do [*Hamlet*] in St. Joseph's gardens at the end of the summer term, we asked Nan Thorogood to direct because of her new approach to Shakespeare. Now she stood among us, wearing a trouser suit and a black high-necked jumper, her hair scraped back and tied with some sort of bootlace, her high, pale forehead wrinkled with distaste for the wimpish Dane. I had wanted to hug her and vow eternal devotion when she selected me for the lead. Now my confidence ebbed away like tepid bath-water as she explained the reasons for her choice. It had nothing whatever to do with my modest success as Oswald.

"Do you think Shakespeare thought of Hamlet as a hero? What's heroic about him? He can't cope with his relationship with Ophelia. He can't face up to the basically erotic nature of his feelings for his mother. What the hell is this guy? Is he just the failed central figure of Shakespeare's least successful play? Or is he a repressed homosexual?… Years ago Jean-Louis Barrault played him as a guy in love with Horatio." (This came as a surprise to me and greatly increased my anxiety about the whole enterprise.) "Balls!" Nan lit a Capstan full strength and let us into the secret of Hamlet. "He was in love with Laertes."

"But they hardly ever meet," I dared to remind her.

"Of course they hardly ever meet in the play. Except to kill each other. Don't you find that illuminating?"

We thought this over in silence for a while. Then a plump man called Benson, playing the First Gravedigger, whispered to me, "Are you going to have to kiss Laertes, Philip?"

"Of course he's not!" Nan Thorogood's hearing was exceptionally keen. "The drip would never do anything as positive as that, thank you very much. The point is - and this is something I would like you all to think about - that Laertes is the real star of this clichéd revenger's tragedy. Laertes hears that his father's been killed, so what does he do? Doesn't hang about. Doesn't sit around talking to himself. Doesn't go through a rejection of his girlfriend - which is nothing more or less than ritual rejection of all women. Gets on his bike and comes straight home to be revenged! In fact he behaves like a man and not a mouse in mourning. Oh, by the way, you won't be wearing black, Philip. Not in my production."

I wondered, later, what I should be wearing. "You'll be dressed like you are. That old tweed jacket, with leather patches, you've nearly grown out of will do… You don't imagine you're going to camp about in doublet and hose, do you? Speaking the stuff as though it were poetry?"

John Mortimer. *Dunster.*

Suit the action to the word, the word to the action...

ACT 3, SCENE 2.

John Gielgud *who as a director was famous for ever changing his mind, gives notes to the cast of Richard Burton's Hamlet. New York, 1964.*

To Polonius (Hume Cronyn):
It's a bit spry, Hume. Younger than springtime. Try using a cane tomorrow night. I know you'll loathe it, but it might work out well, there's a good fellow. Otherwise, it's beautiful. Truly.

To Laertes (John Cullum):
John, dear - you must not scurry about in the first Court Scene that way. You're the son of a Prime Minister, a personage at court. You must never scurry - you must *stride.*

Cullum explained that he had to negotiate a swift path all the way from extreme stage left to extreme stage right in order to arrive in his final position before the entrance of the King and the Queen. In other words, as he put it, "I have a long way to go." To which Gielgud replied, "Of course, darling - we **all** do."

To the Captain (Philip Coolidge):
Coolidge, it's a charming performance, but get yourself a hat. I couldn't tell you why, but you're nothing without a hat.

To First Grave-Digger (George Rose):
George, dear, it was frightfully bad tonight. Can't bear you chuckling at your own jokes and all that early music-hall biz. Wind in the puss and high fatuity. Do change it.

To Ophelia (Linda Marsh):
At the beginning of your Mad Scene, as you pace idly along the parapet's edge humming your woebegone song, I would like you to loose your footing and drop into Horatio's arms. Once free of him, you should slink about the stage doing something serpentine and gorgeous.

To Hamlet (Richard Burton):
Really splendid tonight, Richard - I must tell you that. The entire section we spoke of from "To be or not to be" through the Nunnery Scene was excellent - I almost liked it.

A few nights later, some of the notes went as follows:

To the Captain (Philip Coolidge):
Charming performance, Coolidge, but the hat doesn't suit you. Get rid of it.

To First Grave-Digger (George Rose):
Superb, truly. I don't understand what you do at all, but you do it awfully well.
To Laertes (John Cullum):
Can you possibly get to your position faster during the first Court Scene? We're all waiting for you after the King enters.

Cullum explained that he was trying to seem more dignified as per Gielgud's suggestion. "Of course you were," Gielgud replied. "But be dignified faster."

To Ophelia (Linda Marsh):
As you broke away from Horatio tonight, you went slinking about the stage doing a number of interesting movements. They were adequately serpentine but not altogether gorgeous.

Gielgud: When Alec (Guinness) said to Ophelia in the play scene, 'That's a fair thought to lie between a maid's legs,' he reached right up her skirts in front of the whole court.
Burton: Well, John, that's good for Alec, but I'm liable to get a sexy reputation.
Gielgud: I could add a programme note.

William Redfield. *Letters From An Actor.*

By Cock, they are to blame.

ACT 4, SCENE 5.

Joseph Papp, the American director and producer who founded the New York Shakespeare Festival in 1954 and the Public Theatre in 1987, produced an anti-Hamlet in 1967 which caused quite a lot of controversy.

The guards wear GI uniforms, Claudius the dress of a South American dictator, Gertrude appears in negligées and Ophelia in miniskirts, singing her rock dirges into a mike, dressed like a go-go girl in a straw hat and tights.

Hamlet is first seen emerging from a coffin which sits at the foot of Gertrude's bed, reading "Oh, that this too, too sullied flesh" at breakneck speed, with no inflection whatsoever. He wears boxer shorts while standing in the audience throwing peanuts at the stage.

Robert Brustein.

Express our duty in his eye.

ACT 4, SCENE 4.

Kenneth Tynan reviews the performance of Michael Redgrave *when he played Hamlet at Stratford in 1958.*

Sir Laurence Olivier once said he would rather lose his voice or his arms than his eyes. Watch Mr Redgrave's: no matter how he rolls them about, they remain somehow glazed and distant. We know from the evidence of our own that he has two of them, yet something about him persistently suggests the Cyclops. They are 'simply things in his dreams'. Try as he may (and God knows he tries), he cannot establish contact with us as human beings. Just as we think he's about to break through to us, something within him shies and bolts. He withdraws into his solitude, and when next we look, the windows are shuttered again.

Kenneth Tynan.

Olivier is a *tour de force*, Wolfit is forced to tour.
Hermione Gingold.

Is there not rain enough in the sweet heavens...

ACT, 3 SCENE 3.

Laurence Olivier first played Hamlet in 1937 at the Old Vic for Tyrone Guthrie - which was played in its entirety - the production being transported a few months later to a rain-sodden Elsinore. Tyrone Guthrie remembers affectionately the occasion.

Elsinore was no picnic. The performances were arranged by the Danish Tourist Board and were to take place in the courtyard of Kronborg, a seventeenth-century castle on the sound which divided Denmark from Sweden.

We had sent over plans of the stage set and a list of requirements for rehearsals, dressing-rooms and so on. We were assured that all would be in perfect order and that, for good measure, we should have the full co-operation as "extras" of a hundred of the Corps of Officer Cadets who were quartered in the castle.

We arrived a week before the performance. The Cadets were perfect - a hundred blond and intelligent young men ready to do or die in the service of art. A stage set had been built to the design of a Danish artist, who was considerably huffed when we insisted that the use of his set would involve rearranging the entire production, and that the whole thing must be rebuilt in precise conformity with our plans. More serious was the fact that the authorities in control of the castle had never been informed that we needed to rehearse.

The castle was open to visitors all day and the authorities were not prepared to close it. Accordingly we rehearsed all night. Even this arrangement was rather upsetting to the authorities, who were convinced that theatre was in some way synonymous with fire; reluctantly they permitted us to rehearse from midnight until six in the morning, but insisted on our employing a large posse of elderly fireman in steel helmets with axes in their belts. Since the courtyard is made of stone, with walls at least a foot thick, and since the weather was exceedingly wet, the precaution seemed excessive, but the firemen did us no harm and seemed, dear old things, to enjoy the play.

In these rehearsals, although it was pretty cold in the small hours and we were often soaked through and through, we would find ourselves full of energy at the end of a long night; the great problem was not how to keep awake, but how in the freshness of a May morning to commit what seemed the sacrilege of going to bed and trying to sleep.

Miss Baylis was in her element. Like a good commander she shared the hardships of her troops. Night after night she sat through the rehearsals, dispensing from a window sandwiches and lemonade. We used to break for twenty minutes at about three in the morning: the company and the cadets and the orchestra - military musicians resplendent in skin-tight, sky-blue uniforms with silver lace. One night the rain was more persistent and more violent than ever before. Miss Baylis was not at her usual window, but in a sort of porter's lodge, and word got round that she had laid in a keg of rum. Came the break and with it an ugly rush towards the porter's lodge. At the head of the hunt was the colonel who commanded the band.

"Not you!" screamed Miss Baylis in the raucous tones which Englishwomen reserve for foreigners who, naturally, are stone deaf, "Not you!" and we just heard a resounding whack on a sky-blue behind. "You're just band. This stuff's for *my* people."

The opening was to be an important occasion - the Tourist Board had left no stone unturned. Royalty was to be present; a special train had been chartered to convey the royal party and the diplomatic corps from Copenhagen. The press was there in force. And that night it rained as never before.

The performance was at eight; at seven-thirty the rain was coming down in bellropes. Miss Baylis, Larry Olivier and I held a council of war. It was out of the question to abandon the performance, indeed the special train had already steamed out of Copenhagen. To play in the open air was going to be nothing but an endurance test for all hands. We would give the performance in the ballroom of the hotel. There was no stage; but we would play in the middle of the hall with the audience seated all around as in the circus. The phrase hadn't yet been invented, but this would be theatre in the round.

The audience thought it a gallant effort and were with us from the start; actors always thrive on emergency and the company did marvels. But *Hamlet* is a very long play. After two hours of improvisation the actors became exhausted and a little flustered. The finale was a shambles, but not quite in the way the author intended. Still it had been a good evening; royalty looked pleased, ambassadors clapped white-gloved hands and the press next morning acclaimed a "sporting gesture" and a *Hamlet* of more than ordinary vitality.

The performance would have worked better if we had been permitted to use all the entrances to the hotel ballroom. But one - the most effective one, a double door at the head of a short flight of steps - was strictly forbidden. The head porter, six foot six, in frock coat and brass buttons, was obdurate. "This door cannot, it must not, it will not open." Ours not to reason why; besides, there was no time for argument. The reason emerged next morning. I asked the man, who seemed a reasonable and friendly person, why he had been so firm. "I will show you," he said, and tiptoed down a veranda towards the double door. In the architrave sat the nest of a pair of blue-tits; the little hen, nervous but gallant, fluttered about our heads. "If this door had been used, she would have deserted her eggs; you wouldn't have wanted that."

Tyrone Guthrie.

Olivier's Hamlet was the best performance of Hotspur that I have seen.
James Agate.

Never make known what you have seen tonight.

ACT 1, SCENE 5.

John Osborne *describes, in the first volume of his autobiography, how he played and directed Hamlet with his Hayling Island Repertory Company, during the summer of 1954.*

I cut the play down to a running time of a little over two hours and threw myself into the part in manic defiance of the other dismayed actors and their mincing theorizing. It was a superb opportunity to express my contempt for them through Shakespeare...

Ophelia, a vapid virgin from Leicester, no less, who had won prizes at R.A.D.A., asked me to leave her bedroom. As for Gertrude, I had quite capriciously decided to my own satisfaction that she was a prying lesbian who had prevailed on Ophelia to reject my attempts on the body she coveted herself. In the closet scene, I mauled her as lewdly as her costume allowed, which still gave me some clinical opportunities...

As a Hamlet, it was a passable impersonation of Claudius after a night's carousing. I looked forward to Gertrude slapping my face during the scene or at least walking out afterwards. She would have been eagerly supported by the other actors on artistic if not moral grounds but, like them, she seemed almost intimidated by the low, lunging coarseness of the Osborne Prince, a leering milk roundsman of Denmark Hill, full of black looks rather than nighted colour. Seldom can a Hamlet have exemplified so wholeheartedly the vices mocked in the speech to the Players.

Anthony [Creighton] managed to remember a smattering of the Claudius I had left to him. I was almost unaware of the others. They were interruptions of a huge euphoria I was certain never to be allowed again. I persuaded the local schoolteacher to send some children, and about a dozen bought half-priced tickets. Some of the retired folk from the Victoria Hotel and their friends walked the few yards into the theatre. There could never have been more than thirty altogether. They were patient and possibly too infirm to hobble out. One old gentleman told me I reminded him of Frank Benson but that I was much noisier.

Mrs. Creighton came proudly to watch her son's valiant attempts to drop his lines on some random target. She had somehow persuaded my own mother to see the last performance. Understandably, she was bored. She had accidentally seen the Olivier film, not knowing in advance that it was Shakespeare. "I've seen it before," she said to Mrs. Creighton, meanly giving away the plot. "He dies in the end." She thought my peroxided hair made me look a bit of a nancy boy and too thin. Watching the home audience and the surly embarrassed actors at the one scrambled curtain call, she said loudly, "Well, he certainly puts a lot into it." And, with a sigh, "Poor kid." It was unusually prescient.

John Osborne. *A Better Class of Person.*

I could see the puppets dallying.
ACT 3, SCENE 2.

Hamlet performed by Nathan Evans, Edinburgh Festival, 1996.
Reviewed in The Stage by Gerald Berkowitz.

Though not a very good puppeteer, he uses puppets. Though not very good at different voices, he uses different voices. Though not very good at acting, he acts his little heart out. The sight of him wrestling with himself while playing both parts in the Nunnery Scene, or the sound of him singing "What a piece of work is man" with two handpuppets, is enough to turn you off live theatre forever.

Such bugs and goblins in my life...
ACT 5, SCENE 2.

A live television broadcast of *Hamlet,* sometime during the mid-1950's, overran quite considerably. The result being that the end of the play had to be replaced with a Kiora orange squash commercial. Sir Lew Grade, then head of Independent Television, rang up the station in a blind fury demanding to know "What the hell happened?" "Well", said a rather tired voice, "I'm afraid they all died in the end."

Till then in patience our proceeding be.
ACT 5, SCENE 1.

The mad scene: apart from the lines, much better Barbara - I can tell you're getting more used to the straitjacket. Oh - any news on the skull, Connie? I'm just thinking, if your little dog pulls through, we'll have to fall back on papier-mâché.

Victoria Wood. *Up To You Porky.*

How absolute the knave is…
ACT 5, SCENE 1.

Richard Burton, the Frank Sinatra of Shakespeare.
Elizabeth Taylor.

And you, the judges, bear a wary eye...
ACT 5, SCENE 2.

Richard Burton *first played Hamlet in 1954, at the Old Vic.*

Winston Churchill attended a performance one afternoon and sat in the front row with a copy of the play, which he followed out loud. In the interval he went back stage and knocked on Burton's dressing-room door...

"My Lord Hamlet, would you be so kind as to permit me to use your lavatory?"

Heaven and earth, must I remember?
ACT 1, SCENE 2.

After he had seen his performance Gielgud came around to Burton's dressing-room to take him to dinner and observing, he was beset with visitors, said, "Shall I go ahead Richard, or wait until you're better - I mean, ready?"

No one now to mock your own grinning.

ACT 5, SCENE 1.

June Whitfield once played Hamlet in the BBC radio comedy series Take it From Here opposite Jimmy Edwards's Gertrude and Alma Cogan's Ophelia. The narrator was Dick Bentley.

JUNE: Oh, what a rogue and peasant slave am I,
   I'll help my mother bake an apple pie.

DICK: Hamlet puts down the sequin skull he's carrying and looks around the stage.

JUNE: Now, don't forget all you children in the audience, if you see the Ghost, all shout out 'Look behind you, Hamlet!' And the little boy and girl who shouts the loudest will get a Hopalong Polonius badge!

ALL: Look behind you, Hamlet!

DICK *(laughs)*: This is very amusing. The Ghost has just popped out of the pantry on a unicycle and disappeared into the larder. Now Hamlet calls his mother, Queen Gertrude.

JUNE: Mothah! Mothah!

JIM *(as Dame)*: Here we are, here we are, all girls together, Queen Gertrude herself - "They call me Dirty Gertie 'cos me jokes are Danish Blue." Oh girls, what a day I've had! What with that wicked Claudius pouring half a pint of 'ot lead down my old man's lughole - well, I ask you! I've hardly had time to rinse out my soliloquies. Now where's that lad of mine? Hamlet, where *are* you!

JUNE: I'm here, mother. Oh, mother dear, I'm in love again. And this time I know it's going to be a success.

JIM: A success! I'd say it's more likely to be Ophelia!

DICK: Hamlet and the Queen go into a soft shoe shuffle - when suddenly the door opens and in staggers Ophelia herself, soaked to the skin and carrying a bunch of rosemary.

ALMA: Turn again Hamlet, Prince of Denmark!

JIM: Angels and Ministers of Grace defend us!
   Ophelia! Soaking wet and on her benders! –   What happenethed?

ALMA: Thou knows't the willow which grows askant a stream?

JIM: I wot it well.

ALMA: I tripped over it.

JIM: You mean you've been - ?

ALMA: Yes, I've been - altogether - everybody!

ALL *(sing)*: Floating down the river on a Sunday afternoon…

Frank Muir and Denis Norden. 1954.

Suit the action to the word...

Act 3, Scene 2.

David Warner played Hamlet in 1965 at Stratford for the R.S.C. directed by Peter Hall. He was, in a sense, plastic material in Peter Hall's hands as Warner had never seen or read the play. And you can't come to it fresher than that...

When David Warner was performing Hamlet one evening, a member of the audience actually entered into the play. It was near the end of the second act, just after Hamlet dismisses Rosencrantz and Guildenstern. With a sigh of relief, Warner breathed, "Now I am alone." He raked the stalls with his eyes, scooping in the balcony with a wide look, and then began the soliloquy: "O, what a rogue and peasant slave am I..." At the series of short questions, beginning with "Am I a coward?" Warner paused, just to think about what he'd said. Surprisingly, one of the spectators shouted, "Yes!" Warner responded, "Who calls me villain, breaks my pate across/ Plucks off my beard and blows it in my face/ Tweaks me by thy nose, gives me the lie i' th' throat/ As deep as to the lungs? Who does me this?" And now a name was shouted out from the audience! Warner was excited and responded with some vehemence, "Hah, 'swounds, I should take it; for it cannot be/ But I am pigeon-liver'd..."

Warner remembers this as one of the most exhilarating nights of his acting career.

Mary Maher. *Modern Hamlets & Their Soliloquies.*

David Warner - R.S.C. Stratford. 1965.

Hamlet is idiotically sane
With lucid intervals of lunacy.
W.S.Gilbert.

HAMLET.

My wife was as good could be
Until twelve months ago,
About that time we went to see
The famed Lyceum show.
Irving there play'd Hamlet,
'Twas a fine performance - but,
Since my old woman 'spotted' him,
She's gone clean off her nut!

At night time, as I lie in bed,
When in a peaceful doze,
The fit comes on, and then she
Fairly spoils my night's repose;
She fancies she's a spirit,
And not solid flesh and bone,
But that's all wrong, for my old girl
Weighs just on eighteen stone!

Last night, to tell the truth, it was
The worst of all the lot,
For as the clock was striking twelve
Clean out of bed she got;
Downstairs she crept upon her toes,
Wrapped in our only sheet,
And in her ghostly garb she walked
Clean out into the street!

Written and composed by Charles Williams. 1920s.

An ill phrase, a vile phrase... but you shall hear.

ACT 2, SCENE 2.

Nicol Williamson stopped the performance the other night and said, "I can't go on - I am simply exhausted, and I'm not giving you my best. In fact I'm fucked..." and then walked off the stage. Well I don't think that's got much to do with acting.

Kenneth Williams. *Diaries.*

How long will a man lie i' th' earth ere he rot?

ACT 5, SCENE 1.

It was formerly customary to make the Gravediggers in Hamlet comic characters, and all sorts of tricks were effected for that purpose. Among other comicalities, it was held sacred that the first Gravedigger should wear an indefinite number of waistcoats.

Edward Wright was the first Gravedigger and Paul Bedford the second. When they were about to commence the operation of digging the grave for the fair Ophelia, the chief began to unwind by taking off waistcoat after waistcoat, which caused uproarious laughter among the audience. But as the chief digger relieved himself of one waistcoat, Paul, the boy digger, incased himself in the cast off vests; which increased the salvos of laughter, for, as number one became thinner, number two grew fatter and fatter. Wright, seeing himself outdone, kept on the remainder of the waistcoats, and commenced digging Ophelia's grave.

Jacob Larwood. *Theatrical Anecdotes.*

Rich gifts wax poor when givers prove unkind.

ACT 3, SCENE 1.

Nicol Williamson *played Hamlet in 1969 for Tony Richardson.*

Admiring Nicol, I wanted to do something with him in the theatre. I had never staged *Hamlet*. I felt there had been no major revaluation of the character since the legendary 'poetic' Hamlet of John Gielgud's in the 1930's. It seemed an ideal role for Nicol, and I longed to explore the play.

When it opened in February 1969, *Hamlet* was an enormous hit and received international plaudits. Nicol was recognised as his generation's Hamlet; without illusions, yet humorous and ironic, capable of instant rage and mockery, and with a sad, existential resignation. He too was erratic in performances and walked off or interrupted the show several times - to the consternation of the stage-management and company, but to the titillation of audiences, who loved to participate in these kinds of drama temperament. Worse, he soon was away over the top in his own acting and reckless of other people's feelings. Soon after the opening, he was already overacting shamelessly, although he didn't know it. I attacked him for it. He never forgave me. But in the early days, when he was good, he was terrific.

Tony Richardson. *Long Distance Runner.*

O what a noble mind is here o'erthrown!

ACT 3, SCENE 1.

It was during a matinée at the Royal National Theatre in September 1989 that Daniel Day-Lewis underwent a phenomenal experience.

At the moment in Act 1 when Hamlet suddenly confronts the Ghost for the first time, Daniel Day-Lewis, having lost himself so completely in the character, found that he was staring not into the eyes of David Burke who was playing the dead king, but into that of his own late father. The effect was so catastrophic that he was powerless to continue with his performance. He quickly and quietly left the stage, never returning to the part again.

Too Much Hamlet.

I went to book a ticket for to see a modern play;
The man behind the counter said, 'There's no such thing today,'
Every actor who has any self-respect is being starred
In the brightly-written masterpiece of England's Only Bard.

It's 'Hamlet' here and 'Hamlet' there,
And 'Hamlet' on next week.
An actor not in 'Hamlet' is regarded as a freak.

A pleasant farce with music would, I thought, be to my mind,
But not a single pleasant farce with music could we find.
At every theatre which I sought men answered with a bow,
'We've given up our farces. We are playing "Hamlet" now.'

It's 'Hamlet' this, and 'Hamlet' that,
And '"Hamlet" - Mr Jones.'
Our starving British dramatists are mainly skin and bones.

I went into a music-hall, but soon came out of it
On seeing some comedians in a painful 'Hamlet' skit,
And a gentleman who gave some imitations, all alone,
Of other people's Hamlets, plus a Hamlet of his own.

It's 'Hamlet' this, and 'Hamlet' that,
And 'Hamlet' day by day.
Shakespeare and Bacon must regret they ever wrote the play.

I don't deny that 'Hamlet' has its merit as a play:
In many ways it's finer than the drama of today.
But with all respect to Bacon (and his colleague) I protest
That I think the British Public is entitled to a rest.

It's 'Hamlet' here, and 'Hamlet' there,
And '"Hamlet" - Record Run'.
It seems to me the masterpiece is being overdone.

P.G. Wodehouse.

Most like a gentleman.
ACT 3, SCENE 1.

John Gielgud is now completely and authoritatively master of this tremendous part. He is we feel, this generation's rightful tenant of this 'monstrous Gothic castle' of a poem… I hold that this is, and is likely to remain, the best Hamlet of our time.
James Agate. 1944.

The rest is silence...

ACT 5, SCENE 2.

The critic James Agate was watching an open-air production of *Hamlet* in Regents Park when he heard a small boy behind him say to his mother, "Mother, I'll tell you when I'm bored with this - and it's now."

For this relief much thanks. ACT 1, SCENE 1.

ACKNOWLEDGEMENTS

Clive Francis would like to thank the following for permission to reproduce copyright material. Every effort has been made to trace and contact all copyright holders but he apologizes for any errors or omissions and, if informed, would be glad to make corrections in future editions.

Alec Guinness and Hamish Hamilton Ltd, *Blessings in Disguise.* (Copyright Alec Guinness, 1985).
John Gielgud and Hodder & Stoughton, *Backwood Glances.* (Copyright John Gielgud, 1989).
    Early Stages, Macmillan. (Copyright John Gielgud, 1948).
John Mortimer and Viking, *Dunster.* (Copyright John Mortimer, 1992).
The Estate of Tony Richardson and Faber & Faber, *Long Distance Runner.* (Copyright The Estate of Tony Richardson, 1993).
The Stage newspaper and Gerald Berkowitz for its review of the Demarco Foundation, Edinburgh Festival. (Copyright Gerald Berkowitz 1996).
Macmillan Children's Books and The Estate of Richmal Crompton, *William the Pirate.* (Copyright The Estate of Richmal Crompton).
The Estate of Anthony Quayle and Barrie and Jenkins, *A Time To Speak.* (Copyright The Estate of Anthony Quayle, 1990).
J.M.Dent, *Moody Dane* from *Nine Sharp & Earlier.* (Copyright The Estate of Herbert Farjeon).
Joss Ackland and Hodder & Stoughton, *I Must Be In There Somewhere.* (Copyright Joss Ackland, 1989).
Hamish Hamilton, *A Life in the Theatre.* (Copyright The Estate of Tyrone Guthrie, 1960).
Random House for Robert Brustein's *The Third Theatre.* (Copyright Robert Brustein, 1960) and
    P.G.Wodehouse's *Beerbohm Tree* from *The Green Parrot and Other Poems,* 1907).
Michael Parkinson and the BBC for an extract from the Peter O'Toole interview.
Kenneth Branagh and Chatto and Windus, *Beginning.* (Copyight Kenneth Branagh, 1989).
Mary Z. Maher and Iowa University Press, *Modern Hamlets.* (Copyright Mary Z. Maher, 1992).
Frank Muir and Denis Norden for an extract from *Take It From Here*, BBC 1954.
Ray Galton and Alan Simpson for an extract from *Hancock's Half Hour*, BBC 1961.
The Estate of Tallulah Bankhead and Gollancz, *Tallulah.* (Copyright Laurence Pollinger Ltd).
Guy Boas poem *Chocolates.* Reproduced by permission of Punch Ltd.
Miles Kington for permission to reproduce an extract from Punch. (Copyright Miles Kington, 1980).
The Estate of Emlyn Williams for an extract from *George.* (Hamish Hamilton Ltd, 1961).
Faber & Faber for an extract from John Osborne's A Better Class of Person, 1981.

Every effort has been made to locate the owners of copyright for extracts included in this book, but not always with success.
Acknowledgement is therefore necessary to the following, or their heirs, from whom we would be glad to hear:
Donald Wolfit: *First Interval* (Odhams, 1955); William Redfield: *Letters From An Actor* (Viking, 1966);
Seymour Hicks: *Hail Fellow Well Met;* (Staples. 1949) and *Between Ourselves* (Cassell, 1930); Frank Benson:
My Memoirs (Ernest Benn, 1930); H. Chance Newton: *Cues and Curtain Calls.* (Bodley Head, 1927).

INDEX